HIP-HOP,
INC.

SUCCESS STRATEGIES
of the
RAP MOGULS

HIP-HOP, INC.

SUCCESS STRATEGIES
of the
RAP MOGULS

DR. RICHARD OLIVER
TIM LEFFEL

THUNDER'S MOUTH PRESS

HIP-HOP, INC.
Success Strategies of the Rap Moguls

Published by
Thunder's Mouth Press
An Imprint of Avalon Publishing Group Inc.
245 West 17th Street, 11th Floor
New York, NY 10011

AVALON
publishing group incorporated

Copyright © 2006 by Dr. Richard Oliver and Tim Leffel

First printing March 2006

Library of Congress Cataloging-in-Publication Data is available.

ISBN: 1-56025-732-6   MAY   2008
ISBN 13: 978-1-56025-732-5

Book design by India Amos, Neuwirth & Associates, Inc.
Printed in the United States of America
Distributed by Publishers Group West

To Jill
Who taught me that a smile is the best bling of all.

To Donna and Alina
For helping me remember it's not all about the Benjamins.

CONTENTS

INTRODUCTION
Music, Message, and Money

HIP-HOP, INC. **TELLS** the inside story of a unique group of African American entrepreneurs who are rewriting the book on entrepreneurship in American business—selling black culture to white audiences, rather than selling white culture to black audiences, or even selling the black experience to just their own community. For the first time anywhere, *Hip-Hop, Inc.* reveals the success strategies and management principles of the hip-hop moguls who are blazing a new road to the American dream.

But wait, hasn't this story already been told?

No. In fact, a book exclusively about the business of hip-hop is long overdue. There are volumes of glowing, positive material available about the history of rap and hip-hop, about its traditions and its stars. An almost equally sized quantity of materials exists about and by detractors. Only incidentally, and then in gushing but not very enlightening anecdotes, are the business aspects of hip-hop even discussed. And then it is usually about the wealth: the cribs (homes), wheels and rims (cars and fancy wheels or hubcaps) and, inevitably, about the bling (expensive jewelry and accessories).

The genesis of the idea for the book grew out of frustration about this dearth of material about the hip-hop business phenomena. Rick Oliver is a business school professor who tried—to no avail—to find information about hip-hop business successes in order to share with students the story of a new, modern business model ... and, honestly, to try to appeal to students with subject matter of real interest to them.

Finding little information, the idea of a book about the hip-hop businesses, and the entrepreneurs who created them, was hatched. Although the book was never conceived to be about the music per se, it quickly became evident, however, that real expertise from the music industry was required. Thus, the writing partnership was formed. Tim Leffel holds a music degree and worked for many years at a music label, at times with responsibility of promoting early rap acts such as Kool Moe Dee, Too Short, KRS-One, and A Tribe Called Quest. And so a writing partnership and a book were born.

Hip-Hop, Inc. was written for three audiences:

- ❍ Established businesspeople who need to hear the story of one of the most exciting, engaging, and insightful success stories of our times;
- ❍ Academic business audiences, faculty and students alike, who need a case study of a successful new way of doing business;
- ❍ The *new American entrepreneurs* (who, as we'll describe later in the book, are for the first time both black and white, young and old, men and women, immigrant and long-time citizen).

We trust that it will serve both the intellectual curiosity of the academy and the practical desires of the business world.

A Walk on the Dark Side

Talk of aspiring entrepreneurs leads us to the greatest difficulty we faced in writing this book: what to do about rap's dark side. Some rap music was created in less than savory, or legal, circumstances. Many of its lyrics openly promote violent crime and misogyny.

Few businesses escape some negative press. Rap is no exception. But while most traditional businesses steadfastly avoid

negative attention, many rap impresarios and artists seemed to
seek it out, to revel in it. In fact, for a while it became an integral
part of the business. Deliberate or incidental, the fact remains
that rap had, and still has, a dark side. The East-West rap rivalry
generated bitter disputes and even a few notable deaths. Some of
the moguls have been sent to jail more than once. Not the stuff
of business role models.

One of the rappers killed was Tupac Shakur, clearly one of the
most creative, gifted performers of any genre. Likewise, one of
the early West Coast rap entrepreneurs, Suge Knight, is, by all
accounts, a gifted individual. But his brutal tactics and illegal acts
resulted in his experiencing jail time and the loss of a budding
empire. Even as this is written, he is surrounded in controversy,
having been shot in the leg at a party before the 2005 MTV Music
Video Awards.

In the end, we decided to briefly include the story of the dark
side, not as a model to emulate, but as an object lesson in wasted
potential. On balance, we believe that the dark side is part of life,
of business, and should not be swept under the rug. As Chuck D
of Public Enemy famously said, "Rap music is the black CNN."
At its worst, it serves to demonstrate the thin line between good
and evil; at its best, it serves to highlight the large and truly positive side of hip-hop.

As we worked with business and music librarians to understand
what had already been written about hip-hop, and interviewed
many people in and around hip-hop, our constant refrain was:
"It's not about the music, it's about the business." We weren't
always successful getting the message across. So we'll try one
more time.

Hip-Hop, Inc.: It's Not About the Music

We tried to remain faithful to this idea throughout the book:
at its core it's about business. Intuitively, however, we knew
the music was important. What we didn't know, though, was

how central to the business the music really is. Not because it supplies the capital to start the related businesses, but because everything about the music—origin, attitude, style, packaging, personality, lyrics, and beat—sets the context for, and definition of, the business. The music of rap and the business of hip-hop are inextricably linked. It's a new music with it's own fundamentals, but it touches the same emotional core in its audience as music has done for many millennia. Hip-hop is a new business form operating on tried-and-true, age-old business principles, but with a new set of clothes.

Wait. Hold the Ringtone. It *Is* About the Music!

We started out wanting to write about the hip-hop game—the business, not the music. What we found was that the lyrics and beat of the business closely paralleled that of the music. So, more than we ever imagined, this is also the story of the music, music that, as two middle-aged white guys, we have come to know, understand, appreciate, and even love. Consequently, the story of the music is told alongside the story of the hip-hop business.

While we came to know the music and the business of hip-hop, decoding the language was a special challenge.

Secret Code?: Nonstandard English

English is the world's most dynamic and comprehensive language, adding thousands of words annually. It is a wonderfully rich language accommodating new and ever-changing ideas, technologies, motives, emotional situations, diseases, and the human condition, and just about anything else you could imagine.

In writing about technology and business, our usual "beat," we have noticed that new words are a defining characteristic of not only new technologies, but also the people who create and use them first. Fifty years ago, words such as *chip, megabyte, cell phone, wireless, download,* and even *computer,* were not within the common vernacular. Today they're part of everyday speech. Likewise acronyms such as *CPU, iPod, MP3,* and *DVD* roll easily off the tongue.

One of us once sat in a bar with a friend who was a computer hardware designer and five of his colleagues in the same industry. For five minutes straight, he had no clue what the computer guys were talking about. "Sorry about that," one of them finally said, sheepishly. "It's hard to turn off the 'chip talk.'"

In the early stages of a new technology, newly coined words, old words given new meanings, expressive phrases, acronyms, and the like are used by certain groups almost as a secret code. The inventors and their close-knit group of kindred souls use distinctive words to define their group: only those in the group know the meaning, others are excluded. Excluded, at least until the words become part of the standard spoken and written language. It allows the group to *name and claim* the intellectual territory, so to speak. With information technologies (computers, telecom, and even digital audiovisual devices), the "techies" maintained virtually exclusive control of the technology and the products until everyone else cracked the code.

In that context, hip-hop is no different. As *Music in East Africa* author, Gregory Barz, showed us (see chapter 3), hip-hop is a lineal descendant of West African music that most often contained secret code words to convey messages to groups outside the political authority. Anyone who has listened to any rap knows that hip-hop has a language all its own. It invents new words and phrases (*bumrush, homie, crunk*). It gives new meaning to old words (*hard-core, chronic, peeps*). And it uses standard words in new and different contexts (*dead presidents, buck-fifty, pimp juice*). Mostly, though, hip-hop takes basic, standard English words and phrases and renders them nonstandard. A good example is this from 50 Cent ("Like My Style," from the album *Get Rich or Die Tryin'*):

On ya mark, get set, let's go, switch the flow
Teach ya how to turn yayo in to doe
The original don dada nobody bomb harda
Ya heard what I said boy, I'm hot, I'm hot
The hoodrats they say "He so crazy"
The snitches they say "He tried to spray me"
Well, that's what you get for tryin to play me
The Aftermath and my wrath is so SHADY
No matter how you try you can't stop it
I catch ya stuntin in the Bentley Coup Cockpit

Such rich and creative use of language has many uses, the exploration of which is beyond this book. One thing is clear though. The words definitely send a message to the "in crowd"—those who know the meaning and the context of the language—and it excludes those who don't. At once, it defines a culture and gives it definition and cohesion. Most importantly, from an economic perspective, it creates the opportunity to deliver an entire set of lifestyle products to those who know the language and its meaning, and to those who wish they did.

This book occasionally uses the nonstandard idioms of hip-hop for emphasis and effect. With a diverse readership, the authors of this book are sensitive to the fact that everyone may not know certain business expressions and words. Where the message is unclear, we provide a brief, bracketed definition of the word or phrase with its first use. Even this is difficult, though, because the meaning of many of these expressions is changing constantly. The word "bling-bling," for example, morphed into just "bling" during the writing of the book. The language changed so fast, in fact, that one magazine, *Hip-Hop Connection*, billing itself as the genre's oldest publication, includes a section called "New Slang." A 2005 issue explained, for example, the term "slab": "Slab is an old school car, one with candy paint, a popped trunk and the swangers we ride around on are the fo-fos. That's the type of rims they are. It's a car that's fixed up."(So now do you get it?)

Despite the challenges, we hope the book will act as a "protocol converter" from hip-hop to business and back!

A central question we faced at the outset of our writing was distinguishing between the terms "rap" and "hip-hop." As it turns out, we often use them interchangeably in the book. Not every reader will be happy about that, however. As we found out, there are some pretty strong feelings on the subject.

Rap or Hip-Hop?: The Medium Is the Message

There is no universally agreed upon definition of either "rap" or "hip-hop." Many people use the terms interchangeably, but the most popularly expressed difference seems to be that rap describes a musical style born in the late 1970s in the predominately black, urban culture of the South Bronx, New York City. The style was poetic, beat-centered, repetitive, and featured some artist styles that had never been heard before. In general terms, rap is the musical part of the larger hip-hop lifestyle. The *Harvard Dictionary of Music* offers the following definitions:

> Rap is "a style of music that arose in the South Bronx in New York." Ensembles consist of a DJ mixing sounds and "one or more MCs (masters of ceremonies) who rhythmically declaim spoken rhymes."

> Hip-Hop "denotes the practices of an entire subculture." A part of "the B-Boy subculture that rap and DJs were integral parts of" also including break dancing and graffiti.

A keen observer of the culture is Atlanta-based social activist and entrepreneur Rodney Sampson. He parses the subtle disparity between hip-hop and rap. "It is critical," he says, "to note the difference between the artists involved in rap and hip-hop. Some examples of each: Kanye West is hip-hop, Eminem is a rapper, and 50 Cent kind of straddles the fence. *Essentially, rap music is a well-capitalized stepson of hip-hop that was cultivated by the engine of mainstream music."*

As rap aged into hip-hop, the message of the medium changed dramatically. Rap was the message of youthful disgust and dissent, sent from the street to the silent majority. Many of the rap artists, of course, are still firmly in that mode. Hip-hop, on the other hand, is rapidly evolving into the message of empowered consumerism from the newly economically enfranchised urban trendsetter to their suburban counterpart.

A relatively new magazine, *America*, backed by mogul Damon Dash (profiled in chapter 8), is self-described as "over-sized, super-sexy, platinum-leafed glossy." In describing the hip-hop audience to potential advertisers, it says:

> 30 years ago, hip-hop culture was a gritty, inner-city youth movement. But the hip-hop generation has become the driving force in today's worldwide pop culture . . . the hip-hop nation has matured and succeeded—and is enjoying a lifestyle of fame and fortune . . . [with] upwardly mobile young men and women . . . Urban culture is one of acquisition; a culture measured not just by what you have but how much you have, and who has the best . . . The "bling-bling" ethos is alive and well . . . successful young men and women with a lust for only the finer things and the discretionary income to get what they want.

Emotionally Charged Words: Hurt or Heal?

Much of rap and hip-hop uses extremely emotionally charged words, referencing groups and individuals on the basis of their sex, sexual-preference, race, ethnicity, religion, or job function (i.e., the police, courts, record company executives, etc.). While the old children's ditty "names will never hurt me" may hold true, we have chosen to avoid the use of such words wherever possible.

Some may consider this a "cop-out." The purpose of the book, however, is not to explore or explain, condone, or condemn such language. The purpose, rather, is to discover and describe how a new musical form was converted into a lifestyle and in the process created an entire new industry that has prospered around the world, providing jobs and invigorating a group of heretofore neglected entrepreneurs.

The story of the business of hip-hop is a wild ride, one we hope you'll enjoy.

1

THE GAME

Reapin' Rap's Riches

Hip-hop's the game, helped a lot of brothers escape
Take it to another level, knowI'msayin?
It's our music, we own this music, knowhutI'msayin?

—LL COOL J
"Hip-Hop," from the album *Mr. Smith*

The Game

This book is about "the game": the multimillion-dollar businesses at the center of the multibillion-dollar global hip-hop industry. It is a story being told for the first time from a strictly business perspective. Although rap music and hip-hop cultural products (clothes, jewelry, cars, financial services, publishing, travel, etc.) now dominate many of their product and service categories, this book is not about the music or the bling. There are plenty of books, articles, TV shows, and even movies that do that well. *Hip-Hop, Inc.* is about the businesses that the music and the bling *created*. And it's about how those businesses now create even more music and more bling.

Hip-Hop, Inc. tells the story of how the businesses were founded and why they are so successful. More interestingly, though, it describes the people behind (or in many cases, way out in front of) the businesses, as well as the principles and practices they've used to become so phenomenally successful. The financial success of hip-hop should be of more than passing interest to anyone in business solely on the fundamentals alone. They are truly remarkable: multimillion-dollar empires with global reach, selling a huge variety of products to some of the most desirable demographics (young, high income, acquisitive, interested in luxury products). These empires own brands that are rapidly approaching icon status, most developed in just the last decade or two.

Hip-hop artists and entrepreneurs often refer to the hip-hop business as "the game," but unlike a fleeting sporting event, they recognize that the rules are unforgiving, the personal and professional demands unceasing, but the potential rewards are staggering.

An African American First:
"helped a lot of brothers escape"

In a country of firsts and in the business arena, where innovations are the name of the game, hip-hop represents a genuine watershed in American and even global business. It is the first (legal) industry to rise like a phoenix out of the urban poor of America and has become not just a cultural phenomena, but an industry that generates predictable revenues and earnings, employs thousands, and daily touches the lives of billions of people around the globe.

The hip-hop entrepreneurs are not the first African Americans to create their own businesses, even on the scale that they have. There are those such as Robert L. Johnson, who created Black Entertainment Television (BET), or Cathy Hughes, who created the national radio network Radio One. In the main, however, early pioneers of large, black-owned and -operated businesses were largely oriented to selling the black experience to the black community. Hip-hop is also about selling the black experience to white America and to audiences around the world.

Nor are the hip-hop entrepreneurs the only successful African

American business executives. Black executives, while not found to the extent they should be at the center of Corporate America, are now running such venerable institutions as Merrill-Lynch (Stanley O'Neal, COO), AOL Time-Warner (Richard Parsons, CEO), and American Express (Ken Chenault, CEO). But many of these black corporate executives—like their white CEO colleagues—are the product of America's best schools and country clubs. Many of the hip-hoppers, by contrast, while not from the ghetto, grew up "one street over."

Although they often cultivate a "ghetto origin" as part of their image, many, like Russell Simmons, Kanye West, and Diddy, grew up in middle-class homes with parents in the professions. Some even "flirted" with private schools and universities. Some of the artists and entrepreneurs, such as Tupac Shakur, Snoop Dogg, Suge Knight, Master P, and 50 Cent, came from the poorest parts of urban America and lived what rappers refer to as the "thug life." 50 Cent (or "Fiddy" as he's often referred to) even boasts "eight gunshot wounds" as an integral part of his persona. Impressively, the most successful hip-hoppers were able to translate their street smarts into business smarts with amazing ease.

"Take it to another level, knowl'msayin?"

Hip-hop growth and development is so much more spectacular when considered in the context of the competition for the "cultural dollar" of some of the world's most entrenched suppliers (Sony, Viacom, Calvin Klein, Electronic Arts, Pernod Ricard, Giorgio Armani, etc.) in each product category in which it competes.

The music industry, though driven by hits and new artists, is in many ways an old-line conservative industry, set in its ways and dedicated to its unshakable genres: pop, rock, easy listening, country, jazz, and classical. Over the past few decades, only hip-hop has made a lasting dent. Along with country music, it now dominates the sales charts.

The same may be said of other product categories, such as

upscale clothes and jewelry, where established brands and producers dominate a very mature industry. Again, while "the newest fashion" is the de rigueur operating mode, at their core these industries rigidly protect their turf and reject innovation from the outside. A few new designers do break in, but before hip-hop came along you could be sure none of them came from the South Bronx.

Strategic Inflection Point:
"We own this music, knowhutI'msayin?"

The big break, the big idea, the turning point (or as business professors would say, the *strategic inflection point*) for hip-hop, came from a single idea: own the music!

Owning your own music had been done before, but only on a limited scale, with big, established names like Frank Sinatra, the Beatles, and Ray Charles. But owning the rights to your own music virtually never happened (and still doesn't) with upstart new acts, especially those with a radical music genre and really strange-sounding names. In the history of the pop music business, few artists have successfully fused commercial artistic success with entrepreneurial achievement.

But just owning the music doesn't guarantee success. Probably the only one who reached superstar levels at both in music's golden age was Frank Sinatra, "the Boss of the Boards," who *Variety* reported in the late 1950s and early 1960s "STRADDLES SHOW BUSINESS LIKE A COLOSSUS" as a singer, Academy Award–winning movie star, nightclub performer, and record executive. Sinatra founded his own record company, Reprise, in the early 1960s after placing twenty-three hit singles on the charts at Capitol Records.

Unlike Sinatra and the hip-hop moguls, however, most singers have historically failed miserably when they tried to venture far beyond the recording studio or the concert stage. Their musical gifts seemed mutually exclusive to business acumen. The Beatles, the most successful and influential band of the rock era, proved themselves inept as entrepreneurs when they ambitiously but naively launched their own multi-platform brand called Apple Corps, Ltd., in London in late 1967. A few months later Paul McCartney and John Lennon appeared at a rare news conference in New York (the band had last performed live at San Francisco's Candlestick Park eighteen months earlier), where they launched into a rambling diatribe somewhat typical of those psychedelic days. The setting was perfect—aboard a Chinese junk floating in New York Harbor. John Lennon told the reporters that Apple's goal was to explore "if we can get artistic freedom within a business structure, to see if we can create things and sell them without charging three times our cost." Paul McCartney made a telling comment as well, saying that he and his three bandmates "were in the happy position of not needing any more money, so for the first time the bosses aren't in it for the profit. If you come and see me and say, 'I've had such-and-such a dream,' I will say, 'Here's so much money. Go away and do it.'"

The Beatles opened an Apple Boutique on London's Baker Street. An avalanche of tapes, films, poems, and plays from showbiz hopefuls and other eccentrics arrived at the boutique, encouraged not only by the news conference but also by the band's advertisements in the British musical trades asking unsigned musicians to mail tapes to Apple Music at 94 Baker Street, London W1. The result was a short-lived but unmitigated disaster.

Hip-Hop: Got the Message

Atlanta-based black intellectual and entrepreneur Rodney Sampson, a keen observer of the hip-hop moguls, explains the difference between earlier black entertainers, who, he says, have always operated on a "work for hire" basis, and the new breed of hip-hop moguls, who, again according to Sampson, have applied the principles of business ownership and leadership with staggering success. He draws a bright line between the two when he says,

"The *rappers* work for hire, while *hip-hop artists* own their work."
He goes on to explain: "Why did 2Pac [Tupac Shakur] really never
own any successful corporation outside of the advances he was
being paid by the record labels? It goes back to the work-for-hire
mindset and the entrepreneurial mindset."

Sampson's insights into the rise of the moguls are extraordi-
narily valuable, as he is a highly connected member of the African American intellectual and business community in Atlanta,
where he shares the half-spiritual/half-entrepreneurial appeal of
the moguls. Sampson's first full-time position after receiving his
MBA from Penn State was as second in command at Mt. Carmel
Baptist Church, with some twelve thousand members.

Sampson has applied his MBA training and leadership skills
to found and run several influential companies that embrace and
spread the message of the moguls' business ethos worldwide. One
of the business entities he runs is the Living Legacy Foundation,
an organization with the specific purpose of training one million
leaders around the world in hip-hop and popular culture.

The contrast between rap and hip-hop is a stylistic distinction
between musical directions and influences that may seem subtle
or obscure to whites, but that is crystal-clear to African Americans. When Sampson speaks of rap and rappers, he does so with
little enthusiasm; when he speaks of hip-hop artists and moguls,
he does so admiringly. "I have also seen the positive influence of
hip-hop music and culture in Africa and Europe," he says. "Its
influence has transcended, and will continue to transcend, to the
corporate boardrooms throughout the continents."

The early hip-hop crowd recognized the intrinsic value of
ownership, had the guts, or "extreme confidence" (as hip-hop
impresario Damon Dash has been described as possessing), and
drew the line at ownership. As Smokey Fontaine, editor and pub-
lisher of the glossy hip-hop magazine *America*, says, "Guys like
Damon recognized intuitively what many others couldn't see, or
didn't want to see, or weren't allowed to see: that you get rich four
times faster at 50 points [by owning the rights and allowing the

record companies to do the distribution] than you do at 10 points [a royalty rate when the record company took ownership of the recorded music and the artist received 10 percent]."

In his book *Life and Def*, Russell Simmons describes an early epiphany on this point after having his "first hip-hop experience": "'The real revelation for me was the 'world famous' Eddie Cheeba rhyming ... it really got me excited ... I felt I was witnessing the invention of the wheel. I was standing in a room full of peers ... and it hit me: I wanted to be in this business." Simmons instinctively knew at that moment that the key to success was control. As he did his first deals, he held his ground on ownership. And when he did, he changed music, black America, entrepreneurship, fashion, and entertainment, and in the process spawned a whole new industry.

Russell Simmons was still "on the street" when he recognized what he had to do. An old saying goes, "I'm not sure who discovered water, but I'm sure it wasn't a fish." Like a fish in water, Simmons was immersed in the music and the culture. His contemporaries didn't recognize what was happening. Simmons did. His genius was (and still is) that he recognized what most of us don't because we're too surrounded by it to understand.

Jeff Clanagan, who ran Master P's film company and now heads up Code Black Entertainment, says the hip-hop entrepreneurs always have a major advantage over big, entrenched companies. "I pay attention and keep my ear to the ground. Big company people like to sit in the office."

The music of hip-hop, both the lyrics and the beat, are straight from the street. They are often full of angst, anger, and allegory. The beat is hypnotic, the words strangely expressive and evocative of a way of life, a human condition, or a cry of anguish. Laced among the words of sorrow, despair, and resignation, however, are words of hope, encouragement, and direction—as hip-hop superstar LL Cool J says, *"own the music."* Like so much of the hip-hop lyrical form, it's secret code for: own your business; take control of your own life.

For the hip-hop entrepreneur, the time had come to seize control. This is their story.

> Looking to take over the world is my goal
> With my unstoppable crew takin' all control
> You can't get none of this, we're runnin' this
>   —LL COOL J
> "B Real," from the album *Mr. Smith*

Fly: Takin' Over the World

Whether or not Russell Simmons started out with the idea of taking over the world, he along with Jay-Z, Damon Dash, Eminem, Diddy, Missy Elliot, LL Cool J, Kanye West, 50 Cent, Master P, and a host of other well-known and not so well-known (yet) hip-hop entrepreneurs seem very much on their way.

Hip-Hop, Inc. is the business story behind the music and culture. It's about business principles and practices, strategy and vision, execution and commitment, branding and positioning, and about pricing and profits. You won't find any discussions in these pages as to who is the best rapper or the best producer. In some sense, the music is just the accompaniment to the story. The music provided "the juice" (respect and power) to make the business story possible.

Telling a story is what hip-hop music is all about. So, in fact, is business. Most ads for products tell a story. Most prices tell a story (about what it cost to a make product and what its perceived value in the market is). Balance sheets tell a story, as do cash flow and profit and loss statements. Each year, publicly owned businesses file millions of documents with the Security and Exchange Commission (SEC) and publish annual reports to shareholders that tell a story (or as some critics would argue, just purport to tell a story).

So where's the story of the business of hip-hop? Not where we expected to find it! And we looked and looked and looked. Everyone in business knows that the first place to look for the inside story—in some cases the only place to look—is the Harvard Business School. So we started there.

Yo, Harvard: Where's the Cases?

For more than fifty years, America has trained its new management elite on another uniquely American invention, the "business case study." In its simplest terms, a case study is merely a history of a business situation, written for business students to study, debate, and understand what went right and what went wrong. While a number of other schools have invaded their territory over the last several years, the business case owes it origin to Harvard's prestigious business school (widely known in business and academic circles simply as HBS). Today, literally thousands of HBS cases, used by millions around the world, cover every conceivable company of size or business situation of importance.

Harvard's case studies cover the world of business success and failure intensively and extensively. Type in any Internet business term or dot-com founder's name in HBS's exhaustive search engine (www.harvardbusinessonline.hbsp.harvard.edu), and you'll get dozens of hits. But type in Russell Simmons, Jay-Z, Damon Dash, Master P, or Puff Daddy, and you'll get . . . nothing. Try alternate names: Sean Combs or Percy Miller. Nothing. Type in rap, or hip-hop, and still get nothing. Not one case, not one history. Nothing.

In many ways, *Hip-Hop, Inc.* is the HBS business case that's yet to be written, the business case for the hip-hop moguls. It's their story. The story of their dream . . . a uniquely American dream, and a dream finally, at long last, being dreamt in black and white!

Defiant. Tough. Profane.
Branding. Positioning. Profits.

The words of rap music are often irreverent but the beat is always hypnotic. The results are pure gold.

Hip-hop has captured a world's imagination and turned profane street slang and hard living into a global phenomenon. Related products are earning billions of dollars annually in clothes, financial services, cars, movies, jewelry, and a host of other extensions. The hip-hop industry has created cultural icons with strange-sounding names, who convert ghetto-ized lyrics into mountains of bling. In many ways the bling says, "We've made it!" But in other ways, because it's often oversized, outrageous, and overdone, it serves as a message that its been made *in spite of* traditional mores and values and sets hip-hop apart from the mainstream culture. Bling, like hip-hop, is different and defiant.

Many entertainers and sports figures have used a special aka, or nickname, to brand themselves, or to "name and claim" a position in the public's eye. Many have done it before: The Sultan of Swing, and The Babe in baseball; Shaq in basketball; The Great One in hockey; Broadway Joe and The Fridge in football. Some of the earliest of such names accompanied professional wrestlers, who in the beginning of the twentieth century went by such handles as The Strangler, Killer, and even a woman wrestling champ named Moola (because it was said, "she was all about the money"). Other prominent users in the public eye were members of the Mafia: Baby Face, Scarface, and Pretty Boy Floyd. Recently, even prominent businesspeople have gotten into the act: The Donald, Neutron Jack, and Chainsaw Al.

But the hip-hoppers have taken the aka name game to new heights. Instinctively, they recognized the value of the brand and the nature of positioning. Their names conjure up something illusive, forbidden, exotic, erotic, and often, wealthy:

Snoop Doggy Dogg
OutKast
Rush
Notorious B.I.G.
Eminem
Public Enemy
LL Cool J

Dr. Dre
Ludacris
Kurupt
Slick Rick
Beastie Boys
Puff Daddy
50 Cent
Suge Knight
Silkk the Shocker

**Market Share. Cash. Fortune.
Irreverence. Infamy. Insolence.**

What's in a name? Perhaps no hip-hop handle names the game
like 50 Cent. The name is money. Small, silver pocket change for
one very large, black multimillionaire. The first artist since the
Beatles to have four hits at once on the top ten singles chart, he
sports eight scars from street-fight bullets. With a torso covered
in tattoos (personal graffiti) and clothed on stage in little more
than rags, he's captured endorsements, international acclaim, and
more than fifty million dollars for a career that only started in
2002. Perhaps his signature album, and the hip-hop anthem (at
least from a business perspective), is *Get Rich or Die Tryin.'*

Maybe it's ironic, but 50 Cent owes his start to another rapper of sharp contrasts, Eminem. A white star in a traditionally
black genre, Eminem has owned the charts, made millions, and
wreaked havoc as a social outcast. He also had the business sense
to sign 50 Cent to his own label.

Like the names, are the rappers authentic? Or are they just
part of the show?

Authentic. It's a word you hear often when Russell Simmons,
the godfather of hip-hop, talks about the music. It comes from
the 'hood, it bleeds real blood, it grits because it's straight from
the gut. And that, perhaps more than anything else, is the reason
for the global success.

Street Smarts. Guts. Raw Talent.
Customer Focus. Cash Flow. Contribution Margin.

> If I can't do well, homey, it can't be done
> Now I'ma let the champagne bottle pop
> I'ma take it to the top
> Fo sho I'ma make it hot, baby (baby)
> I'm the drop out who made more money than these
>   teachers
> Ruthless like the Coupe but I come with more features
> I am whut I am, you could like it or love it
> It feels good to pull 50 grand & think nothin of it
>   —50 CENT
>   "If I Can't," from the album *Get Rich or Die Tryin'*

When Disney-owned music label Lyric Street opened its doors in July 1997, Randy Goodman was named its president and has been there ever since. Before heading up Lyric Street, Goodman was the number two executive at RCA Records' New York headquarters. His duties included overseeing the marketing of the Jive Music roster and the launch of eventual rap superstars the Wu-Tang Clan. Goodman and senior vice president Doug Howard have combined to provide Lyric Street with steady leadership and a growing market share, through a period of major challenges and rampant contraction and consolidation within the music industry.

Goodman (the father of several children, including an eleven-year-old son who helps him stay in touch with hip-hop) says: "I've always been impressed by Russell Simmons and Diddy. At Disney we are painfully aware that kids' tastes are a moving target, but when I was growing up, rock 'n' roll was the music of rebellion. Now my son brings home records by rock artists like Green Day, and I understand that music. But with hip-hop, kids' parents have no clue what it's about. It has lyrics that bother and offend them, and it has warning labels on the CDs. The parents don't get it, and that makes the kids *more* interested in it."

What about the business sense of the moguls? Goodman says, "Russell and Sean have a unique entrepreneurial spirit. Dr. Dre has done it, too. These guys seem to do things at a level that most people don't understand. They have an innate sense of how corporations work, and a real gift for determining when to go street and when to be corporate."

Where did that knowledge come from, that rare gift of street smarts and corporate vision? "The successful selling of their music," Goodman concludes, "taught them how to develop their other corporate brands."

"I think what happens with people like Sean Combs and Russell Simmons is this: they came from the street," says Goodman. He witnessed some of hip-hop's earliest breakthroughs right at the source, when pioneering rap acts were hawking cassette singles on the streets of Brooklyn for pennies. "That's where hip-hop was born. These guys have great intuition and a superb sense of what's going on. Even though they're powerful now, this commercial success hasn't kept them from being hip and cool. Far from it."

Cool, yes. Hip, no question. Street smart, yo! But more than anything else, the distinguishing characteristic of the most successful hip-hop moguls is simple: hard work. A secret? No. It's right there in the instructions.

Instructions to Assembling: Aspiration vs. Inspiration

> I got my back against the wind
> I'm down to ride 'til the sun burn out
> If I die today i'm happy how my life turned out
> See the shoot outs i done been in them by myself
> Locked up I was in a box, by myself
> Ida made myself a millionaire, by myself
>
> —50 CENT
> "Heat," from the album *Get Rich or Die Tryin'*

Many entrepreneurs and executives in "the game" lament that people are not getting the whole story when it comes to making money and seeing success. In his song "The Food," rapper Common laments that kids only see the results of the success, not how it happened. "Shorties get the game but no instructions to assembling."

"It can't be all about consumption," says Kenny Burns, one of the founders of the RyanKenny fashion line and the head of a growing music business empire based in Atlanta. "We're way too *aspirational* and not *inspirational*. You have flashy videos and everyone is rich and the kids say, 'I want that!' And they want to go *straight* to that; they don't understand that there's a process in between. Rappers like Common and Kanye West are putting the whole message out there. They talk about living out their dreams, but working very hard to do what they want to do."

"We always look at the leaders and not the workers," Burns adds. "But you can never have a bunch of leaders alone. It's hard to be a leader: they are creative and strong and give direction. But nothing happens without the workers. Nothing gets built."

Jeff Clanagan says a lack of understanding of the hard work required also permeates American movies and television. "Either everybody's bling-bling or everybody's a comedian," he says. "The kids see the images on TV, but they don't see the work that it took to get there. They don't know the process behind it."

In Kanye West's song "Touch the Sky," he talks about going from broke to bling, buying fancy jewelry from Jacob the Jeweler as soon as he got his advance from the record label. Jay-Z, the older mentor, tries to set him straight:

> I went to Jacob an hour after I got my advance.
> I just wanted to shine.
> Jay's favorite line: "Dog, in due time"

For either of our audiences, successful businessperson or aspiring entrepreneur, *Hip-Hop, Inc.* aspires to the "instructions to assembling" a new business in an era dominated by new technologies and new business rules. The first chore in that quest is to understand the game.

> I don't care what it did to them
> The game's been good to me
>
> —EBONI FOSTER
> "Heavy in the Game" featuring
> Eboni Foster, Lady Levi, Richie Rich from the
> Tupac Shakur album *Me Against the World*

Tupac never lived to enjoy the full measure of success in the game. To debate whether or not Tupac would ever have aspired to, or been inspired to be, a hip-hop mogul is now a useless exercise. Understanding the size and importance of the game, and the moguls who create it, however, is well worth the effort.

2

HIP-HOP'S 'HOOD

America's New Silicon Valley

> . . . if you ain't up on the game
> Then I suggest you rearrange
> Cause change gone come
> And it ain't waitin on no one
>
> —SNOOP DOGGY DOGG
> "Change Gone Come," from the album
> *Dead Man Walkin'*

TO SAY THAT hip-hop changed the game is to state the obvious. But until now, just how it changed the game has been a closely held mystery. Shrouded in tough words, angry music, and often defiant artists and spokespeople, hip-hop has guarded its secrets well. When pressed, the hip-hop moguls talk in circles, speak about results, but do not often divulge their strategy or their tactics easily.

Being close-mouthed about how you succeeded—as opposed to going on at length about the nature of the success itself—is not that surprising. In fact, that's precisely what most businesspeople preach and practice in other industries. But there it's referred to as trade secrets, competitive intelligence, and many other MBA-style euphemisms.

The hip-hoppers, however, are above all else public people. Many of them love to talk: about their bling, their cribs (homes), their posses (entourage), their cars, their videos, and their schedules and workout regimes; but mostly they talk about the music. Seldom, however, do they hold forth about the details of the business. When they do talk business, they only let little snippets of their strategy and style out at a time. Again, it is not much different than smart businesspeople in other industries.

Keepin' It Private

None of the hip-hop businesses has as yet "gone public." They may be aligned with, or distributed through, a company such as Time-Warner, Vivendi, or Sony, but their label successes stay private. Doing an IPO (an initial public offering) dramatically transforms what the outside world knows about the inside of a business. Private companies do not have to disclose information about their operations, organizations, successes, or failures. Public companies, on the other hand, face mountainous requirements to divulge virtually everything about everything. The requirements have become even more consuming, costly, and onerous since the passage of federal legislation in 2002 that is commonly called the Sarbanes-Oxley Act (or Sarbox).

The Sarbox regulations forced more transparency on public companies and further chilled what little was known about private companies. The privates have retreated safely into their shells, thankful that they aren't required to disclose the timely and detailed information that their public cousins do. So maybe the hip-hoppers are just keeping quiet, in the age-old tradition of "closely held" businesses.

A Marcy Projects MBA?

Or it may just be that unlike many of their white counterparts, who learned business terminology around the dinner table, the country club, and in America's best MBA schools, they don't have sufficient business vocabulary to talk about what they do and how they do it.

Jay-Z drives that very point home on his bigger-than-life billboards for Reebok: "I am what I am. I got my MBA from Marcy Projects." And Kanye West built his first album around the idea that he was a *College Dropout.*

When they do toss out some numbers, they often do so to confuse the competition. A *New York Times* article about Russell Simmons's Phat Farm clothing company noted that he routinely inflated the revenues of the company to make the upstart brand seem bigger than it actually was. In a surprisingly open moment, Simmons said in a court deposition: "It is how you develop an image for companies. So in other words, you give out false statements to mislead the public so they will then increase in their mind the value of your company."

So how do you go about understanding the business of hip-hop? How do the leaders of hip-hop businesses actually achieve success? This book is dedicated to answering those questions.

New, But Not So Unique

Ask any businessperson about their industry, and they'll answer: "Our industry is unique, it's unlike any other industry." Ask any businessperson about their company, and they'll answer: "Our company is different, it's unlike any other company."

The truth, though, is that companies are more alike than different and that most industries have particular economic configurations that are commonly repeated in other industries. Further, once any industry's structure is discerned, once key influences and dynamics have been identified, it's relatively easy to plot its growth and change.

As President Harry Truman once said: "The only thing about the future you don't know is the history you haven't read." Truman, of course, was talking about politics, but the same can be said about business. Industry growth and structure are almost always repeatable and therefore predictable. Fortunately, the same can be said about corporate strategy and executive management techniques, the subjects of this book.

A careful reading of the hip-hop history and a diligent tracking of hip-hop business growth reveals repeatable patterns of strategy and recognizable styles of management. The hat may be on crooked, the tie may have vanished, sneakers may have replaced laced-up wingtips, and the leather briefcase given way to a constantly ringing mobile phone, but underneath, business is business, management is management.

As the following chapters demonstrate, all the classic business ideas and practices are in their place in the world of hip-hop. At first glance, the hip-hop moguls' success story seems consistent and simple:

1. Create a popular entertainment brand.
2. Extend the brand to fashion, beverages, or other consumer goods.
3. Use every opportunity to cross-promote the brands—often with what is called *viral marketing.*
4. Collect your money and repeat.

Aspects of solid business principles or management practices can be found with each of the hip-hop moguls. But each mogul, more than the others, seems to uniquely symbolize a particular approach, idea, or principle. What business strategies and management ideas do the moguls epitomize?

Vision, strategic thinking, focus, expert planning and execution, understanding and ruthless exploitation of market anomalies, leadership, market and customer intuition, brand building and positioning skills, and commitment to defining and growing the business "category."

A close examination of their business records reveals that each of the five hip-hop executives who are focused on in this book (Russell Simmons, Sean Combs, Percy Miller, Damon Dash, and Shawn Carter), and many of the other hip-hop entrepreneurs briefly profiled (such as Eminem, 50 Cent, Bryan Williams, Lil Jon, Dr. Dre, etc.), clearly understand the business principles listed above. And each demonstrates, to one extent or another, the successful management styles found in executives of other business.

The most successful moguls show a clear understanding of the key business principles, and each of them exhibit the management skills in abundance. Interestingly, though, each of the five moguls most closely studied seemed to especially exemplify one skill or the other:

Russell Simmons: he has it all, but is particularly adept at vision and leadership;

Diddy (Sean Combs): also has it all, but is a walking, talking brand;

Master P (Percy Miller): brilliant vision to be sure, but flawless execution of every detail;

Damon Dash: intuitive sense of the market opportunities and unparalleled confidence in execution;

Jay-Z (Shawn Carter): defines the term "boss."

All the attributes and attitudes, business strategies and skills listed above are *necessary but not sufficient* to create big new businesses as the moguls have. One more thing is needed. This essential ingredient can be summed up in four simple words: Dream big; work hard.

No dream is bigger than hip-hop, and no group works harder than the moguls.

The *New* American Dream: Black, Hip . . . *and* Hard Workin'

The American Dream: America's gift to the world. More than just a dream, it's a vision. A fully formed vision of the Horatio Alger story: "making it" from rags to riches by creating a multimillion-dollar business that soars to the stratosphere of success. It creates hundreds or thousands of jobs and creates untold wealth for its founder.

A dream, yes . . . a vision, definitely . . . but for one group of Americans it's also been *a myth!* At least until now. For more than four hundred years, the American dream has been at the very heart of the American psyche. The dream. More than anything else, the dream has drawn millions of people to America. Some will argue that democracy and freedom, not wealth, makes America the world's great people magnet. But what value is democracy and freedom if not to let those who wish to achieve, achieve all that they can? It's the *entrepreneur,* the single-minded, creative individual, often obsessed with a dream, and a vision of a great new business idea, that's at the heart of the American dream. It is the mind and spirit of the entrepreneur that makes America the envy of the world. From the daring of the early settlers in the New World, to the modern-day business "start up," Americans display an uncanny expertise in birthing great economic enterprises out of almost nothing but a dream.

But the dream always had a backbeat: the myth that it didn't matter what color, or race, or creed, or sex you were, or even where you were from . . . *the dream was supposed to be open to everybody.* But the reality was quite different. The successful American entrepreneur has mostly been cut from the same cloth: young, white, middle-class, and male. That is, until the 1980s.

Dreamin' in Color

Arguably, America's most inspirational entrepreneurs and its biggest dreamers are the hip-hop moguls. They have created large, enduring companies that define much of the world's, not just America's, new lifestyle and culture. In the space of just two decades, rap music co-opted the mainstream music industry and created one of the most lasting, if unlikely, success stories in American business history.

It's American dreamin' with a new color: the fairy-tale rise of hip-hop entrepreneurs who promote acts that now routinely outsell the biggest rock acts, and whose cultural empires now rival the most successful American icons. Most importantly, their rags-to-riches stories recount the success strategies of these hip-hop moguls who are well on the way to being the first "rap-to-riches" black business billionaires with the power to change the world.

The Belly of the Beast

Rappers refer to jail or equally difficult situations as being "in the belly of the beast." Clearly some of the rap ethos is direct from the belly. While a small number of hip-hop's moguls are portrayed as gangsters—an image that often seems cultivated intentionally—there's no denying that many of them are brilliant entrepreneurs. Some have demonstrated business instinct and marketing savvy that would make many *Fortune* 500 CEOs envious, and many in fact have been ranked among them as part of America's wealthiest elite over the past few years.

According to *Billboard,* four of the top-selling albums of 2004 were by hip-hop artists, while three others featured numerous rap elements or guest stars. In October 2003, for the first time in the history of the *Billboard* top-ten pop singles chart, all ten chart places were occupied by African American recording artists, nine of the ten being rap artists.

On *Billboard*'s year-end pop singles chart for 2004, fifteen of the twenty top singles were from rap artists or had a guest rapper featured. Recorded rap music is now estimated by *Forbes* to be a $10 billion industry, with millions more coming from offshoot businesses such as performances, restaurants, clothing lines, and other hip-hop "cultural" products.

Even the relatively new entrant to the hip-hop game, 50 Cent (a tough persona from the belly of the beast), already has an extensive business empire. It includes a record label (G-Unit Records, a division of Interscope Records), apparel/footwear ventures (G-Unit Clothing and footwear, joint ventures through the Ecko Clothing

Company and Reebok, respectively), vitamin water (Formula 50), a watch line (G-Unit Watches, through Jacob & Co.), and a video game (*50 Cent: Bulletproof,* through Vivendi Games). He openly describes his plans "to dominate the film and television worlds" through two new G-Unit ventures in film and television.

Russell Simmons has joined New York City's business elite and has become one of the richest men in town. Sean "Diddy" Combs, owner and operator of Bad Boy Entertainment and the Sean John Clothing line, and Percy "Master P" Miller, who oversees the No Limit empire, have both ranked among the wealthiest Americans under the age of forty by both *Forbes* and *Fortune* magazines. In 2004 Master P fell off *Fortune*'s list, while Shawn "Jay-Z" Carter took his place.

These larger-than-life figures demonstrated remarkable staying power through the most tumultuous business period in American history—the roller-coaster economic conditions of the last two dozen years. Despite the turmoil in other markets, they created hugely profitable enterprises that endured and grew through good times and bad. Through a combination of old-fashioned business savvy, shrewd marketing, and constant commercial reinvention, the elite rap moguls have prospered.

Even financial magazines have trouble getting a handle on how much the moguls are worth, so the real dollar figures are speculation. But over the past decade, the estimated collective net worth of just five of the moguls grew to more than $1 billion. Given Simmons's comments reported by the *New York Times,* a healthy grain of salt is due, but the net worth figures from the research departments at *Forbes, Fortune,* and others credibly make the case for each net worth:

Russell Simmons: $380 million
Sean "Diddy" Combs: $315 million
Sean "Jay-Z" Carter: $286 million
Percy "Master P" Miller: $210 million
Damon Dash: $175 million

The amounts are staggering. The dream is alive. The stakes are high. So who is winning—and more importantly, how?

How They Got the Juice and How They Keep It

Every one of the moguls has taken a different route to the top. One thing, however, is at the core of every story: hard work. No substitutes. From dawn to well after dark, Diddy seems to be virtually everywhere at once. 50 Cent watches every single detail of everything he touches. Master P is obsessive about being at the center of everything, working nonstop to get it right.

Staring out the window of his palatial office in one of Manhattan's impressive office buildings, Russell Simmons, the original hip-hop mogul, gives up one of the true secrets of his success when he says simply: "Anybody who wants to partner with me has to be prepared to work as hard as I do." Working hard has always been a Simmons trademark, and few can outdo him when it comes to hard work and determination. Few that is, until Russell met Sean Combs.

Sean Combs was competitive from the start. One legendary story says that Andre Harrell, then the head of Uptown Records, introduced a young Sean Combs to Russell Simmons at a New York City gym. A brash teenager, Combs bet Simmons, who is athletic and always in great shape, seven hundred dollars that he could outlast him on the StairMaster. After ninety minutes, Simmons gave up and Combs collected on the bet (which he used to pay for some badly needed repairs on his car!).

Combs's journey from hustling teenager to head of a sprawling business empire is a classic hip-hop version of the American dream.

Sean John: World Domination?

Sean "Puff Daddy" Combs dreams about taking over the world. In reality, he got a good start in 1997:

- His number one album sold more than seven million copies;
- He was artist of the year in *Rolling Stone* (and appeared on the cover);
- He was named producer of the year in *The Source;*
- His breakout single, "I'll Be Missing You," was number one for eight weeks on the U.S. charts and number one in fifteen other countries; Between his own album and the songs from others on his Bad Boy label, fully one-third of the hits that year had the Sean Combs stamp.

Fast-forward a few years to the middle of the next decade, and Sean "Diddy" Combs is well on his way to global conquest. His commercial music success has never returned to quite the level of the late '90s, it will likely be awhile before anyone repeats that dominance of the charts. With a fortune estimated to be more than $300 million, he no longer has to hustle at the StairMaster to pay for car repairs:

- *Inc.* magazine ranked Combs in the "Top-10 Celebrity Entre-preneurs in 2004;
- *Time* and CNN named him one of twenty-five people on their list of 2004's Global Business Influentials. As *Time* said of him: "No other CEO has combined celebrity and smart branding quite like Sean (P. Diddy) Combs, 35, head of the sprawling Bad Boy Worldwide Entertainment Group";
- BET viewers named him "Person of the Year" for 2004;
- He hosted the 2005 MTV Video Music Awards;
- *In 2005 OK!* magazine ran a cover story with blazing headline: "On Diddy's $150M Yacht." (The article went on to explain he had just rented the yacht, the "Christina O," originally owned by Aristotle Onassis, and had the likes of Donatella Versace and British actor Rupert Everett join his family for a cruise around the south of France.)

The yacht trip was out of character for Combs, who never seems to tire of work. The process of empire building and adding on more never seems to wear him out, and there are always more projects in the works. His empire, at least what is publicly known, is described in the chart below.

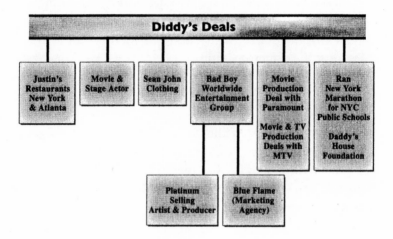

Master P: No Limits

When it comes to hard work, for Percy "Master P" Miller there are no limits. That Master P has vision cannot be denied. But the secret to his success is execution. Master P used his own money and owned everything outright, so he has always been able to do whatever he wanted, with no pressure from the outside. He is an entrepreneur's entrepreneur. He and the other southern moguls who followed have piled up cash by quickly understanding what consumers want and giving it to them. He made a personal fortune by seizing every opportunity that presented itself and going all-out on execution—the hard, unglamorous work of business.

Master P revolutionized hip-hop by bringing a production line approach to music releases and later to direct-to-video movies. He was always watching the bottom line—concerned about what would make money, not what would get on the radio or in magazines, or get him critical acclaim. With Master P it's about the money, not the glory.

Miller got his start as a gangsta rapper with a mean, cutting edge. But he also brought a wholesome family show starring black people to a kids' TV channel and made it a hit. In the process, he has even made his son a star. His hard work goes beyond just commercialism. When Hurricane Katrina ruined his hometown of New Orleans in late August 2005, he was one of the first to show up at the rescue operation.

That's Where the Money Is!

Bank robber William "Willie" Sutton is credited famously (and falsely) with saying, when asked why he robbed banks: "Because that's where the money is." Regardless of the veracity of the statement, what the hip-hop entrepreneurs have discovered is that although they made their start in the music business, it's not where all the money is.

Today there are a dozen or more hip-hop business gurus like Russell Simmons, Jay-Z, Percy Miller, Damon Dash, and Sean Combs, who count their fortunes not just from music, where it all began, but also from a myriad of interlocking enterprises from clothes to financial services. And more are being added by the day.

Francis McInerney, venture capitalist, consultant to many of the world's largest companies, and author (with Sean White, of *FutureWealth, The Total Quality Corporation,* and *Beating Japan*), suggests that the hip-hoppers knew they had to branch out because that's not where all the money is. "The music industry isn't that big. In fact, the Spanish telephone company, Telephonica, has more revenues than the music industry. The music industry alone wouldn't quench the thirst of the hip-hop moguls."

The fashion, clothing, soft drink, movie, TV, auto accessory, and other businesses invaded by the hip-hop businesses are, as they say, "the space above the rim" (hip-hop slang for the highest level).

Above the Rim

The rise and lasting impact of the hip-hop entrepreneur stands in stark contrast to the rise and fall of the Internet entrepreneurs who cost investors more than one trillion dollars! Emerging just before the dot-com craze, the hip-hop entrepreneurs had none of the advantages of the "Internet boys," many of whom were mostly young, white, upper-middle-class, educated, and with lots of "old boy" connections.

As McInerney says, "A great comparison is with the Internet companies that did succeed." Indian and Taiwanese immigrants or first-generation Americans who had a great work ethic and a burning desire to succeed, much like the hip-hop entrepreneurs, started many of those companies. "The most visible of the Internet companies still around today," says McInerney, "like Google, Amazon, and eBay, succeeded because, they, like hip-hop moguls, created a complete customer experience. It takes an enormous insight and effort to create that complete experience."

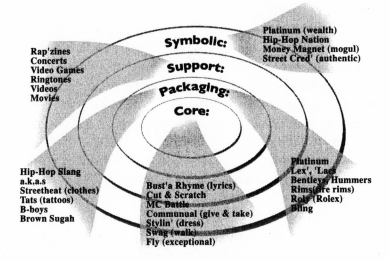

Symbolic:
Platinum (wealth)
Hip-Hop Nation
Money Magnet (mogul)
Street Cred' (authentic)

Support:
Rap'zines
Concerts
Video Games
Ringtones
Videos
Movies

Packaging:

Core:

Hip-Hop Slang
a.k.a.s
Streetheat (clothes)
Tats (tattoos)
B-boys
Brown Sugah

Bust'a Rhyme (lyrics)
Cut & Scratch
MC Battle
Communal (give & take)
Stylin' (dress)
Swag (walk)
Fly (exceptional)

Platinum
Lex', 'Lacs
Bentleys, Hummers
Rims (tire rims)
Rolo (Rolex)
Bling

Hip-Hop: The Total Customer Experience

Some have argued that the dot-com bust was an anomaly. But the Internet boys actually represented the continuation of the traditional American entrepreneurs, and they played by strict establishment rules. The problem was that America and the world had changed while most of the establishment's "old boys" and their "young turk" protégés were looking the other way.

The New America: Wi-Fied, Instantly Messaged, Game-Boy'd, iPodded, and Searchin' for Something to Hold On To

Clearly, the world was hungry for the Internet and the technological lifestyle it engendered. But deep down, young people were looking for something more. Something to define their alienated sensitivities and beliefs in a world depersonalized by technology. It's almost as if the hip-hop moguls sensed that their emerging street culture was the perfect antidote for a new generation, steeped in technological wizardry—Wi-Fied, instantly messaged, Game-Boy'd, and iPodded—but thirsty for a deeper connection to those around them.

The Internet boys in Silicon Valley placed a trillion-dollar bet of other people's money on wild-hair businesses that made no economic sense and disappeared almost as fast as they appeared. By contrast, the hip-hoppers in the South Bronx created global enterprises that employ thousands and have become the new mainstream in business and culture.

Several thousand miles from California's Silicon Valley, and a thousand miles away from New York, the undisputed home of hip-hop, sits Nashville's Music Row. Nearly fourteen hundred companies, large and small, make up the heart of the industry in Music City, USA. In a few square miles, offices of most of the world's record companies, some of its top producers, and reputedly, three-quarters of the nation's songwriters, crank out the hits in the only music genre to seriously challenge hip-hop's status.

The Country and the 'Hood

Many argue that there are only two authentic American music genres today: hip-hop and country music. Country music? As one country songwriter has suggested, "It ain't a country song unless it has heartbreak, trains, prisons, booze, and sex." Well, then, what's rap? Just leave out the trains!

As Toby Keith, one of country music's biggest stars, told *USA Weekend* magazine: "My words come from the street, and their words come from the street. That slicked-up pop stuff doesn't come from the street. Its all pre-fab. Darryl McDaniels [from Run-D.M.C.] . . . said he liked my lyrics and understood my frustration about being an outsider. I'm a huge fan of Snoop. He's a poet."

Ludacris, who recently teamed up with Keith for the magazine's cover story, said, "Rap and hip-hop are about bringing people together to your neighborhood and talking about what happens there. Country music is about the same thing—writing about where you're from."

One leader of Nashville's musical and radio communities is Jeff Green, now the executive director of the Americana Music Association. Green was once the executive editor at the trade paper *Radio&Records.* His weekly column on sales and marketing at *Radio&Records* was indispensable; so is the 1,570-page book he wrote, *The Green Book of Songs by Subject.*

Among the hip-hop impresarios, Green especially greatly admires Sean Combs, saying, "I would say that he is regarded as one of the ultimate tastemakers. He really has his hand on the pulse of the hip-hop movement as well as of pop culture overall. People really have a lot of respect for his ears. He has a Midas touch, with his sense of style and fashion."

Green is particularly impressed with Diddy's remarkable work ethic and emphasizes his emergence as a wonderfully marketable and bankable brand. "For as much money as he's made, he stays very active," Green says.

Sean also surrounds himself with people to help him stay in touch with trends and with the street. Look what he's doing now in terms of producing and A&R ["artists and repertoire," the division within a record company that scouts talent, signs new artists, and picks songs for the existing acts]. He's a brand and he has exploited it very well, and as long as he stays ahead of the trends he'll do very well. I also don't think he's shlocked out, he hasn't gone to the low level. His lines are very prestigious clothing and design.

Country and hip-hop succeed because they don't follow the trends; instead, they recognize an unmet need and create trends. Market trends are what most businesses try to follow. And they do, in crowded herds following the leader. What really takes leadership—to be ahead of the trend and lead the market to you—is something, in business parlance, called "identifying and ruthlessly exploiting market anomalies."

Ruthless Exploitation of Market Anomalies

You'd never catch a hip-hop mogul saying his success was based on the "identification and ruthless exploitation of market anomalies"—even if it were clear that "ruthless exploitation" is a positive rather than a negative thing. But George Stalk would say it. In fact, he heartily recommends it!

A high-profile consultant for one of North America's biggest and best business strategy consulting firms, the Boston Consulting Group, Stalk says, "Sometimes a growth opportunity lies hidden in a phenomenon that, at first glance, seems irrelevant to the business or contradictory to current practice."

Stalk, coauthor with Rob Lachenauer, of the book *Hardball: Are You Playing to Play or Playing to Win*, describes market anomalies as "Idiosyncratic customer preferences, unexpected employee behaviors, or odd insights from another industry—[that] can show the way to competitive advantage, even decisive advantage."

What Russell Simmons, a prototypical hardball player, saw when he looked at the urban culture was a market not being served. Dozens of fashion experts had looked before and saw nothing of interest. Simmons saw nothing but opportunity. Many have followed Simmons's lead with urban wear—like Tommy Hilfiger—but Simmons was the innovator. Most importantly, Simmons led with the keen insight of a hardball player.

According to Stalk and Lachenauer,

> Softball players want to ignore anomalies or try to suppress them because they don't conform to standard practice. Their senior managers usually dismiss anomalies as narrowly based on random events; running a business to meet standard operating procedures is difficult enough without having to account for every deviation that comes along.
>
> Hardball executives, however, relish anomalies. They look for ways to exploit them, asking: What's really going on here? What can we learn from this? Is there an insight that can take our business to a whole new level?
>
> The key to exploiting an anomaly is to expand it from a rare and isolated instance and apply it to a large volume of customers.

When asked where and how to identify market anomalies, Stalk answers simply: "Shop the way your customers shop."

"A Little Bit P. T. Barnum and a Little Bit Lee Iacocca"

Scott Lindy, formerly a senior executive with Clear Channel Radio, now a director of programming for Sirius Radio, believes the quality that made the hip-hop executives so brilliant in their business decisions is the ability to maintain contact with "the street" despite their own great personal wealth. "They have the ability to be this person worth $100 million and live in a guarded estate, but still be in touch with what's on the street. They're still just regular guys. But all of these guys, make no bones about it, wanted to make money and be famous.

"Usually," Lindy says, "once you get it, money changes you. But these guys had the focus, they were street-smart or they had trusted people with the same entrepreneurial spirit working for them. I think what Simmons, Diddy, and some of the others have in common is that they're a little bit P. T. Barnum and a little bit Lee Iacocca. These guys understand the model that they work inside. What Russell Simmons and Puff Daddy did was to maximize opportunities, and they were smart about their business model."

Consultant Stalk could as easily be talking about the hip-hop entrepreneurs when he describes famous hardball business players like Ted Turner (CNN), Larry Ellison (Oracle), Richard Branson (Virgin Records, Air, etc.): "Interesting examples, because those guys very much live their business. They live life with a high level of intensity."

"When people hear the word 'hardball' they sometimes think about lying, or cheating, or pounding competitors with overwhelming force," Stalk says. "But overwhelming force strategies are rarely successful and that's not something we recommend. Very often the indirect attack makes a lot more sense. When you get down to personal habits, there's no need to tightly link playing hardball with being a workaholic, or being overly intense, or aggressive. Some of the most interesting hardball players are not aggressive people, personally. But in business, watch out! They are playing a very tight game and are watching the competitor closely."

One of the hip-hop entrepreneur mantras is to be authentic, to be out there in the street with the customers. Simmons says it best when he says you don't learn the record business "in the building, but out on the street," referring to music executives who stay cooped up in their lush corporate offices.

It's a trait Stalk greatly admires and one that is a key for hardball players. "There's a personal benefit executives gain by talking with their customers and talking with their competitors' customers. Or seeing how their customers shop. Don't have a secretary go buy your stuff. Go out there and be a customer yourself. What you often see is that people make personal adjustments to the business systems that are imposed upon them. The adjustments are anomalies."

At many levels there is a sharp distinction between the well-read business "professional," like the Internet boys, who are up on all the latest business buzz, and those who, whatever their training, never lose their connection to the marketplace. According to Stalk, "The temptation to be distracted is more of a threat than a lack of focus. Organizations get easily distracted. Frankly, business books themselves are one of the leading contributors to distractions. Some book says it's time to go out and hug your customers and then suddenly everyone is out there hugging customers."

Street-Smart Entrepreneurs

Many observers, and some of the hip-hoppers themselves, claim they learned their business instincts by hustling on the street. And it's true for many of them, such as Simmons and Jay-Z. But what's important is not that you're from the street, but that you continue to be connected to the street, and to hone those street skills, not lose them. "It's very hard to find anomalies sitting in a corner office or staying at headquarters. The anomalies don't show up there; by the time they reach there, they've been filtered, or have died out. People in the office are concentrated on getting the job done, as opposed to the exceptions," Stalk says.

Stalk, a hardball player himself, acknowledges that there is another side, and it's an important one. "There's a long list of things that I do, but I never allow those things to take over 20 percent of my time. Pro bono activities, community service—these are all important and good things, but they can't distract from the heart of the matter, which is where 80 percent of the effort should be going. We can afford to do all the other things because we are really focused on the 80 percent and are doing that well."

Atlanta-based Rodney Sampson, founder and CEO of The Intellect Group (with a MBA from Keller Graduate School of Management in Atlanta) and a number of other organizations, agrees. And he sees that spirit in the contributions that Simmons, Jay-Z, and Diddy make to the community.

Sampson is more than a keen observer of the hip-hop entrepreneurs. They are role models for his own business interests. And, like the moguls, he's quietly taking the lead in spreading the hip-hop entrepreneurial philosophy around the world. For example, he's planning a leadership conference in the South West African country of Namibia.

Inspiring the Confidence in Others to Take on the World

The hip-hop moguls have made headlines with their impact on Wall Street, American corporate culture, and the financial markets. At the same time, more quietly, they have inspired many others from their community and from communities around the country to strike out on their own.

Sampson points out that hip-hop's Atlanta connections are no coincidence (see chapter 10 for more on Southern hip-hop). He says, "This phenomenon is larger than just the music scene here. It really started with Atlanta being the crux of civil liberties in America. From there, it was Mayor Maynard Jackson and others who fought for better-paying jobs and business opportunities. So this mindset of *ownership and access* became a way of life for kids growing up in Atlanta. Yes, there are a lot of moguls that live here or own homes of businesses here. Sean Combs owns a restaurant, Justin's, in Atlanta."

First and foremost, Combs and Simmons are true entrepreneurs. They are connected with their community. They understand [that] the value of their activities goes far beyond music, into clothing and fashion. As successful businessmen, they clearly understand the constructs of marketing, networking, and sales—the core components of any business success or failure. Ultimately, they know how to recognize market trends, seize the moment, and connect markets.

Hip-hop is a way of life for these entrepreneurs and all of those who live and breathe this energy. Because of this, the culture transcends through every component of their lives. Common sense kicks in and they begin to create new business models and opportunities, leveraging the same database and distribution systems they have created.

From a global perspective, these leaders understand the power of relationships. There is a symbiotic, co-existing relationship between music and fashion which, of course, naturally includes clothing.

Sampson argues that, "Most black entertainers—and entrepreneurs—in general are nothing more than 'work for hire.' Until recently, many of them did not understand the importance of maintaining some or all of their intellectual properties. Once they began to understand that the producers and the publishers who owned the intellectual property, the record labels, and the distributors generated the majority of monies, the light bulbs went on. More and more, we are seeing a transition from this 'work for hire' to an ownership, and a control, flexibility, and freedom mentality."

How does that paradigm help us explain and understand the boom of hip-hop culture? "Once the music of hip-hop (because hip-hop is more than just music) permeated and exploded into popular culture," Sampson says, "its other viable components such as language, dance, and clothing quickly followed."

Yes, Russell Simmons and Sean Combs have paved the way. However, artists such as Jay-Z, 50 Cent, Jermaine Dupri, OutKast, and the gospel stars Kirk Franklin, Mary Mary, and

Vickie Winans have also begun to leverage their brands to create business opportunities that affect more than just the black marketplace.

Furthermore, hip-hop has been embraced by white America, and not just *suburban* white America. There are hip-hoppers that live in million-dollar homes in town, mid-town, and downtown. The Jewish community has also embraced hip-hop as well. I can remember my undergraduate experience at Tulane University in New Orleans, which has a strong Jewish heritage and attendance. Having grown up all my life in Southwest Atlanta, a middle- to upper-middle-class suburb of Atlanta, I was literally amazed to meet whites, Jews, Indians, and Hispanics that owned more rap and hip-hop music than I did; and this was 1991. To that end, the music has always transcended race, age, and culture.

Global appeal means transcending national boundaries and racial, religious, and ethnic barriers. The hip-hop moguls have clearly achieved a rare breakthrough in global appeal—in music, culture and business. They've made it a whole new game. To best understand the power and appeal of hip-hop, where the new game came from, we need to turn our attention to its historic roots.

3

RAP'S GOT ROOTS

American Bling

Death gotta be easy, 'cause life is hard
It'll leave you physically, mentally, and
emotionally scarred

–50 CENT
"Many Men (Death Wish)"
from the album *Get Rich or Die Tryin'*

THE SECRET OF hip-hop's global success is no secret at all, it is crystal clear: *rap has roots.*

Some mistakenly argue that rap is just the latest offshoot of rock and roll, a derivative, similar to the diversion of hard and acid rock from mainstream rock sounds—in other words, a black sound derivative of white rock. In fact, the reverse is true. More than anything else, rock started as the result of white artists "covering" black music. Rap, on the other hand, has its own roots and its own legs.

Rap is essentially a continuation of a black musical "angst" that goes back centuries and traveled across an ocean and two continents. While rap shares an oral tradition with rock, rap is an entirely new genre, born of its own traditions, and successful because it embodies the music and text of hundreds of years of oppression and dissent. Rap rings true. It is successful, its advocates stress, because it's authentic. In many ways, rap or hip-hop is an entirely new form of music with its own history. It is based not on rock, but on the historical music of protest that characterizes the black experience in America. However, while that's easy to say, it is difficult to prove.

Gregory Barz is an ethnomusicologist and professor of musicology and religion at Vanderbilt University. "To understand black music," he says, "you have to study both the music and the text. Black music, like much of the African American experience, is difficult to trace, because history took away much of the record.

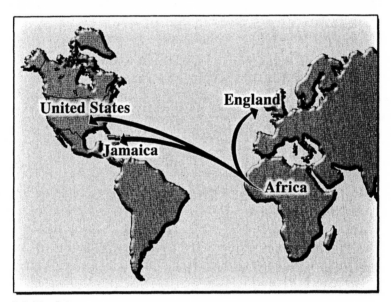

Rap's African Roots

"Anecdotally, though, it is pretty easy to see the rapper as a direct lineal descendant of the 'keeper of the tales' so prominent in the history and music of West Africa. The performance of rap and the culture of hip-hop closely parallel that of Africa."

Barz, who has devoted his career to understanding African music, says,

The traditional "Africanisms" in rap and its performance are hard to miss. The early rap artists honed their craft in live performance, not in the studio. Anyone who has had a black church experience will recognize the form. It is a communal experience, with lots of give and take between the artist and the audience. While traditional rock audiences surely "get the music," the rap audience becomes *one with* the music, a vital part of the experience. It is an emotional, rather than intellectual experience.

Even when they record, there is often a give and take between the main performer and the backup. Not simply repeating lyrics as with many traditional music groups, but deliberate give and take, question and answer, provocative comment followed by an equally provocative response, like you hear with 50 Cent and the G-Unit. And then, too, there's the longstanding hip-hop tradition of inviting other rappers to do cameos on albums and songs. Hip-hop above all else is a communal rather than individual thing, no matter how important the individual artist.

Then there's the competitive element. There is a clear, competitive dimension to hip-hop. Early on was the competing turntables of the DJs and rhyming duels. Then there was the East Coast–West Coast rivalry. Importantly, though, you see the competitive nature of hip-hop most vividly in the text, the lyrics, with challenges to other rappers, to the music industry, to the authorities, and even to audience itself.

An additional common element I see is that not all of the message is evident in the words. While hip-hop seems to have a grammatical form and spelling all its own, there are, like the traditional music of West Africa, hidden messages in the text being subtly communicated to the audience. This is a form of protest delivered secretly to the audience that the authorities wouldn't recognize or understand.

Cultural Chord?

The very core of what Simmons, Combs, Dash, Miller, and the rest of the crowd of rappers turned business entrepreneurs understood, and so skillfully exploited, is that rap touches a profoundly deep cultural impulse. It is an impulse that is not only black, but is the essence of the raw nerve of national, racial, religious, and personal alienation, protest, and dissent found in many places around the world. Hip-hop irritates that cultural nerve as it declares, "I am here, I am important, I will be heard," while at the same time it salves the personal hurt and despair. Importantly for the business of hip-hop, while that cultural nerve was first scratched in the ghettos of New York, it has touched the same nerve around the world.

To understand how a group of inexperienced but intuitive entrepreneurs saw the phenomenal growth potential and pervasiveness of rap, one needs a thorough understanding of the history and geography of black music, from Africa to Afrika Bambaataa.

What is rap, or now hip-hop, and where did it come from? First and foremost it came from the streets of New York and then

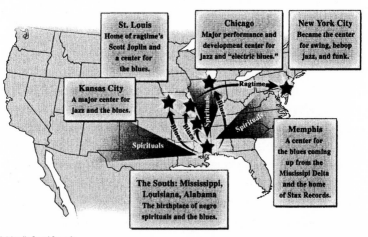

Spiritual's Sound Spreads

LA, of course. While it appeared to the outside world to spring spontaneously from the street, the raw emotions of the 'hood were like a tinderbox ready to explode. Rap was the match that set off the fire. Since the first slave set a bare foot on American soil, authentic black music in America has largely been about protest and escape. Until the rap moguls came along, the story of black music was also a story about struggling to share in the riches.

The story of black music in America has been told many times, and from many perspectives. Its reach and influence have also been argued repeatedly, especially since the history of "black music" and "white music" in the United States have always been inextricably linked. As Arnold Shaw noted in the exhaustive book *Black Popular Music in America*, "Regardless of the social situation and the relations between black and white musicians, our popular music has always been integrated."

The importance of hip-hop and the roots of its remarkable financial success, however, is that for the first time, white audiences are listening to an authentic black sound, not black performers doing white music. As Gregory Barz argues,

> There are notable musicologists who still claim that "Elvis didn't steal black music." But Elvis absorbed the essence of black music as he traveled among the poor black communities and attended black church services in Mississippi and Memphis. While I don't think it was necessarily intentional, there is no question that Elvis "covered" the black sound. More importantly, he legitimized it because young white audiences weren't allowed to consume black music from black artists.
>
> Hip-hop is of critical cultural importance because for the first time in this country, white audiences are listening in great numbers to an authentic black sound from mostly black performers. We now look to black performers for music that truly represents the African American experience, rather than white performers doing black music or black performers doing white music. Today, anything goes. It is fascinating for me to

watch today's college students consume hip-hop and to a great extent black culture. They may not understand the history and traditions that created it, but it really speaks to them.

The Color of Money

In understanding rap in a strictly business context, it matters little whether the color of music associated with Duke Ellington, Elvis Presley, Jimi Hendrix, or Eminem is black or white. What matters is that the recent crop of hip-hop entrepreneurs has found a way to change history when it comes to converting the music into money. The hip-hop moguls have rewritten many financial rules and made sure their money stays in their hands. They've diversified, going beyond the music business to form multiple revenue streams based on selling lifestyle and culture. While the moguls have broken out into business after business, outside music, they started controlling their financial futures with the music itself.

Typically, a recording business held the rights to publishing and to recorded masters. So while the performer's wages were paid per job, the owner of the record or publishing company enjoyed ongoing profits. Although there was blatant cheating and exploitation in some cases, most often artists simply agreed to poor deals. Even today, when a music company holds less leverage than in the past, new artists often get less than satisfactory deals—regardless of race. In the days when black performers were struggling to make ends meet, they were even more inclined to take what they could get. Around 1930, Mississippi blues singer Eddie James "Son" House got his first gig doing a recording session for Paramount. He received forty dollars and reportedly said, "Forty dollars! Making it that easy and quick! It would take me a whole year to make forty dollars in the cotton patch!"

The expansive empires of today's hip-hop moguls are even more impressive when viewed in a historical context. Although, as we'll see, the moguls/rappers are not the first to benefit fully from their own music, they are the first to demand and get the rights to their own music. They are also the first to exploit their position in the business world well beyond music.

Today, the hip-hop entrepreneurs dominate the music world and in many ways the world of fashion, as well as making sizable inroads into many other areas. So what's their story? How did the music with its roots in West Africa come to rule music and business?

The Geography of Rap:
From African Plains to American Plantations

The style of music that traveled across the ocean with African slaves stayed with them, but they typically lacked the means to reproduce it. Pockets of people performed music from the home country on their own, but the genre didn't spread. However, when Christianity took hold for the African immigrants in the early 1800s, "Negro spirituals" became hymns of joyous prayer and a better afterlife. The form also contained coded messages of protest and anger. Spirituals were primarily expressions of religious faith, sung by slaves on southern plantations, but they were sometimes secular-sounding songs with hidden messages and coded warnings about escaping to the north. Most historians trace the birth of American black music to this time, with early gospel music having great influence on the blues, ragtime, jazz, rock, soul, and rap that followed. The "call and response" principle that continued to be so prevalent in gospel, funk, and rap can be directly traced to regions of Africa where slaves originated.

Spirituals also became the first black music moneymakers. In 1871 the Fisk Jubilee Singers went on tour to raise money for Fisk University. Of the nine singers, all but one were emancipated slaves. The attempt seemed foolhardy, but the university was nearly bankrupt and this was a last-ditch attempt to save it. George L. White, the school's treasurer and choir director, launched the project. With the last forty dollars of the school's treasury in his pocket, White took his singers on the road. By the time they performed their way to New York City, audiences started to recognize the singers, who raised thirteen hundred dollars at one church performance—a great sum in 1871. They continued to perform for several more months and eventually met President Grant in Washington, DC. When they returned to school, they presented the university with a check for twenty thousand dollars. Over the next few years their fame spread as they traveled through Europe and performed for the queen of England and the czar of Russia.

Ragtime and Real Money: The Twentieth Century Begins

While spirituals were popular in some concert halls, these songs were generally sung well away from moneymaking opportunities. The only well-paid black performers in the nineteenth century were minstrel singers, also known as "coon singers." In an unbelievably bizarre evolution, minstrel shows started out with white singers in blackface.

Eventually real black singers and comedians started performing in the shows. Some of these performers became famous and even wealthy. As long as there was work, they made a good living. Actor and singer Bert Williams was one of the most prominent, signing a deal in 1914 with a touring company for two thousand dollars a week. When Williams ordered a gin from a bar in St. Louis, the bartender, not wanting to serve a black man, told him it would be fifty dollars a glass. Williams placed five hundred dollars on the bar and said, "Give me ten of them."

Ragtime was the first uniquely American music to become a commercial success. The music preceded audio recordings, but several songs at the end of the 1800s sold more than a million copies of sheet music and were popular in player piano rolls. Scott Joplin and Jelly Roll Morton both became wealthy during ragtime's short run as it progressed into jazz in the early 1920s.

Bring on the Jazz; Start to Swing

Jazz music started in New Orleans and reached Chicago and New York just after 1917. With a young Louis Armstrong on trumpet, King Oliver's band really set off a spark. It didn't take long for jazz to explode, and its influence quickly spread. A black musical called *Shuffle Along* captured a lot of attention as Prohibition started in the "Jazz Decade." In a pattern repeated many times, black music influenced white music of the day, which then affected black music.

Louis Armstrong became and stayed wealthy his whole life, one of the few black musicians to do so. Armstrong made most of his money from acting and performing live, not from royalties or publishing. Count Basie, Duke Ellington, and Cab Calloway rode the swing era to riches by leading large jazz bands at dance halls. One of the most influential black leaders of the era was Louis Jordan, who performed with a stripped-down band called the Tympany Five. The band played in a pioneering style that later became known as rhythm and blues. One of Jordan's singles became a top-ten pop hit in the early 1940s.

Bebop As Black Protest Music

Bebop was the first black protest music, meant to be a backlash against white swing music. Bebop was different. It was intended to be obscure, an "insider's music." Above all, it was meant to be different than the jazz of the time. Some of today's most influential musicians came out of the early bebop era: Charlie Parker, Dizzy Gillespie, John Coltrane, Dexter Gordon, and Artie Shaw.

The insider's music didn't last, however, as bebop eventually became more popular with white audiences than black. Very few performers got rich off bebop, even when their tunes became standards. Artists such as Art Blakey and Herbie Hancock later made more money off royalties from samples being in rap songs than they did from their original recordings. In a way, bebop was a precursor of rap, which came from the streets and was originally music for inner-city kids.

The Evolution of the Blues

Early forms of the blues evolved in and around the Mississippi Delta in the late nineteenth and early twentieth centuries, by musicians using simple instruments like acoustic guitars, pianos, and harmonicas. The blues developed throughout the region, with New Orleans and Beale Street in Memphis being the main urban centers for performers.

The first commercial blues recording came out in 1920, sung by a successful black vaudevillian performer named Mamie Smith. Mamie Smith's story was a typical one; she achieved great riches in her peak, but when the gigs dried up, so did her income. Even though she recorded more than one hundred songs, she died poor.

That first blues recording, "Crazy Blues," was a watershed event for black performers and managers. Its success surprised recording companies, who scrambled to release other "race records." Black-owned record labels sprang up; people started to take them seriously, and both established and new music companies battled over talent. In 1922 fifty blues records were released, and the numbers quickly increased. Many record companies sent "field recorders" with portable equipment to the southern states to find talent. The singers were paid per session, of course, and recording companies earned all later profits.

Another woman by the name of Smith, this time Bessie, was the most successful blues singer in the early days and was universally praised as the best during the ten years she was at her peak. If there had been a richest entertainers list published back then, she would have been near the top. When she was hot, Bessie Smith commanded one thousand dollars a recording session (usually for one song). However, in the days of no royalties, her success didn't last. She died in 1937 with almost nothing to her name.

W. C. Handy of Memphis made the blues an accepted art form. The formally trained musician and composer earned the title "Father of the Blues" by committing many blues songs to notation and creating orchestrated arrangements for bands and singers.

In the 1940s and '50s, blues singers started to earn big bucks. Much of this resulted from amplification, as "electric blues" caught hold in Chicago, Detroit, and Kansas City. Chess Records and its sister label, Checker, were the most successful, signing nearly every Chicago blues performer of note and building up fantastic talent. The label's artists, such as Muddy Waters, Bo Diddly, and John Lee Hooker filled nightclubs and concert halls throughout the '50s and '60s. Chuck Berry took Chess to new heights with a long string of hits and the Rock and Roll Hall of Fame eventually inducted him as one of its first ten artists.

1950s Pop and Rock

Eventually the electric blues led to rock and roll, with black performers Chuck Berry, Fats Domino, and Little Richard. Carl Perkins, Jerry Lee Lewis, and Elvis Presley took the black/white music synthesis in a different direction, fusing soul, rock, and country into a new form altogether.

While it eventually became a white-dominated genre, rock and roll was hardly a white enterprise when it began. In 1951 a Cleveland record shop owner told DJ Alan Freed about some strange purchase patterns in his stores. Teenagers were bypassing the music from Perry Como, Frank Sinatra, and Patty Page to buy records from black rhythm and blues artists. Afraid the term "rhythm and blues" might be too "black sounding," Freed named his radio show Moon Dog's Rock 'n' Roll House Party. The phrase "rock and roll" entered music vocabulary and started to show up in songs, eventually leading to a new genre of music.

Motown Changes Everything

Motown was not the first black-owned music company, but it was the first one to have lasting success. A half-dozen black publishing and recording companies came and went from 1921 to the mid-1960s.

In 1958 Motown Records formed. Berry Gordy Jr. saw Smoky Robinson's band fail an audition, but believed in their talent. Gordy borrowed eight hundred dollars from his family to put out music by Robinson's band, the Miracles, as well as other artists. By 1966 three out of every four Motown releases made the charts, with artists including the Four Tops, the Temptations, Smoky Robinson and the Miracles, Marvin Gaye, Diana Ross and the Supremes, the Jackson 5, Stevie Wonder, and Martha and the Vandellas. Gordy made Motown a completely integrated business operation. He had complete control over the revenue stream as publishing, production, writing, tour booking, and personal management were all handled in-house. In 1967 Gordy owned every share of Motown stock and the company was grossing $30 million per year. By 1972 he was the richest black man in America, with an annual income exceeding $10 million.

Despite all the hits, however, few Motown artists got rich. According to the book *Split Image: African Americans in the Mass Media*, by Jannette L. Dates and William Barlow, David Ruffin of the Temptations lost his job after asking too many questions about finances. At one point the group was being booked at ten thousand dollars per show, but the members were reportedly being paid only five hundred dollars per week. Martha Reeves, of Martha and the Vandellas, says she was never allowed to handle her own finances and earned only two hundred dollars per week. Marvin Gaye claimed he got "$5 a side" for his early recordings. Holland, Dozier, and Holland, the label's successful production and songwriting team, sued Motown for $22 million in 1968 and never worked with the label again.

In 1971 Stevie Wonder turned twenty-one and got access to his royalties, which had been held in trust. He managed to get $1 million out of Gordy, which is an estimated royalty rate of less than 3.5 percent of his sales to that point. Wonder promptly used two hundred fifty thousand dollars to build a recording studio in his home and take artistic control of his music. He was also the first Motown artist to gain control of his publishing rights. He and Marvin Gaye continued to branch out musically while staying under Motown's umbrella. Wonder said, "I'm staying at Motown because it is the only viable surviving black-owned company in the record industry. If it were not for Motown, many of us just wouldn't have had the shot we've had at success and fulfillment."

After Motown moved from Detroit to California in the mid-1970s, it was never the same. The company's $104 million of annual sales in 1982 slipped to $20 million by 1989. However, until MCA purchased it, Motown was the largest black-owned corporation in America.

Motown wasn't the only place cranking out hit records from black artists. Down south, Memphis and Muscle Shoals became hotbeds of both creativity and pop singles. Atlantic Records teamed up with Stax in Memphis and Fame in Muscle Shoals, Alabama, to pump out songs that are now staples on oldie stations. Out of that mix came Percy Sledge, Sam and Dave, Otis Redding, Wilson Picket, and Al Green.

In contrast to Motown's studio "The Hit Factory" and its assembly line, southern soul music was regarded as less slick and gutsier. Arrangements were looser and there was more spontaneity. Most importantly, from a historical perspective, the output was interracial. Nearly all of the pop hits from the era were recorded with mixed-race bands.

Black Music Popularity and the Stirrings of Protest

In 1959 Ray Charles did something nobody thought possible. When he left Atlantic Records and signed on with ABC, he not only negotiated a lucrative royalty rate, but he also convinced the executives to agree to let him keep ownership of his masters. A testament to black music's popularity, the head of ABC/Paramount said, "Whatever Ray Charles wants, give it to him."

Charles knew that his long-term fortune would depend on control of his music. He paved the way for P. Diddy, Master P, Dr. Dre, and Jay-Z as one of the first black music moguls who was also an artist. He amassed enough of a fortune to donate more than $20 million to schools for the blind and established the Ray Charles Robinson Foundation in 1987 for the hearing-impaired. Upon his death in 2004, Charles's estate was estimated to be worth $100 million.

The early 1960s were a golden time for black pop music. In 1962, 42 percent of the year's top one hundred singles were by black artists. (That peak stayed pretty much intact until this decade, when black music singles became so prominent that they took up the top ten spots in 2003.)

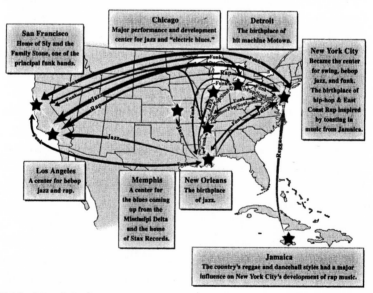

Black Sounds Cross the Country

However, the numbers belie the influence black music of the mid-60s had in parallel to the civil rights struggle. In 1964 Sam Cooke released "A Change Is Gonna Come," a landmark single in terms of speaking up about political issues. Next Curtis Mayfield released "People Get Ready," then Aretha Franklin bowled everyone over with "Respect." James Brown is often credited with starting black pride and awareness in music with his "Say It Loud, I'm Black and I'm Proud." The single shot to number one on the R&B chart and stayed there for twelve weeks.

1970s: Funk . . . and Soul Searching

The mostly feel-good music of '60s Motown gave way to a different vibe. On one end was the escapism of disco, on the other was the socially conscious music in rock and soul. In 1971 Marvin Gaye released "What's Going On," a song that told it like it was, a rarity in its time. It spoke about troubles in the city and protested the numbers of people dying in the war. In 1973 Stevie Wonder's "Living for the City" became one of the first major hits to include both a political message and sampled sounds of the city street. Soul music maintained its popularity with groups such as Gladys Knight and the Pips, Barry White, and Smoky Robinson seeing continual success.

James Brown started funk music at the end of the 1960s. He became known a "the hardest-working man in show business," with a strong work ethic and tight control over his band and finances. He also took music in a new direction, refusing to do it "the way it's done." Unfortunately, he ran into trouble with the IRS and spent much of the next decade straightening out his financial problems.

Others helped propel funk into the mainstream, including Parliament/Funkadelic and Sly and the Family Stone. By 1971 Sly and the Family Stone were so popular that the group got an advance of five hundred thousand dollars per album.

The 1980s: Prince Takes Control

The early 1980s were good to some of the aforementioned acts, but funk really took off when both Rick James and Prince (whose birth name is Prince Rogers Nelson) punched out a string of hits. Prince, however, became the poster child for artistic control, financial control, and diversification. His first step was to rule the creative process. He wrote all his songs, played most of the instruments, did much of the production himself, and eventually built one of the best recording studios in the country. After a series of chart-topping songs and a number one album, he continued to grapple with his record label over finances and control. He performed concerts with the word "slave" written on his face and changed his stage and recording name to a symbol to protest the label "owning" the name Prince.

In the end, Prince showed admirable staying power and a knack for coming back with a vengeance. If he were more involved in hip-hop, he would certainly be included as a subject of this book. He was the number one earner in *Rolling Stone's* Top 50 Moneymakers list for 2004, grossing $56.5 million in one year from concerts and music sales (a good portion of the latter directly through his Web site). He signs only one-album deals with music labels now and still keeps a steady hand on his finances. While Madonna's tour hauled in a higher gross than any other artist in 2004, Prince traveled with twelve trucks of production equipment as opposed to her twenty-four, and cleared twice as much money per show.

The Birth of Rap

The first stirrings of a new black sound came from the New York City borough of the Bronx. It was based on hundreds of years of black American music and thousands of years of its African predecessors. While the black performers throughout American history deserve their place in the annals of the country's musical heritage, the music, musicians, and promoters from the South Bronx were about to touch off a revolution that would belie their humble roots. Although it's tough to judge the lasting social, cultural, and economic impact of the rappers-cum-hip-hoppers while we are still in the midst of their revolution, historians will surely give them their due.

And well they should. As musicologist Barz says, "Hip-hop is the most creative new art form of the past two decades!"

4

THE DOT-COMS BUST

But the Rappers Bloom

Me's a player you know?
I do not, play in no game
Me just, make money, dollars, everytime seen?

—LADY LEVI

Got to the point where I was driven, twenty-four/
seven
Money's my mission . . .

—TUPAC SHAKUR
"Heavy in the Game," from the album
Me Against the World (featuring Lady Levi)

WHEN PRINCE TOOK on his record company over the rights to his music and his name, he really was taking on the music establishment, and maybe in hindsight, the entire entertainment world. More importantly, Prince's protest showed black performers new possibilities through *power of control* in the same way Michael Jackson demonstrated in the 1980s the *economic power of crossover* with his record-setting sales. Michael Jackson's *Thriller* is still the top-selling album of all time. As Bill Adler, publicist for Russell Simmons's Rush Artist Management in the 1980s, said in the book *Yes Yes Y'all,* "When rap first emerged, the only really big crossover artist who was black was Michael Jackson."

South Bronx: In Their Own World

Several personalities are credited with the "birth of rap" as we know it. Whether it was Grandmaster Flash and the Furious Five, Kool DJ Herc, or Afrika Bambaataa who really got the ball rolling, what's not contested is that the music got its start in the Bronx of New York City. Whereas black musicians previously had to have enough money to buy instruments and equipment to get started, rap music could be staged with just a turntable or two, a microphone, and some speakers or an amp. With just some scratching of old records and rhyming over the beats, impromptu concerts were easy to set up, and dance hall jams could feature acts on one bill with no equipment changes.

Kids had few entertainment options in the New York of those days. The discos weren't for them, and in the dilapidated, struggling, drug-running Bronx of the time, very few traditional music acts performed there. Kool Herc started throwing house parties just to give people a place to go, charging twenty-five cents for ladies and fifty cents for men. He would just play funky records and pump up the bass. Herc was an entrepreneur with modest goals. He made his own flyers, rented out facilities, and promoted his own parties, mainly so he could upgrade his sound system.

In the early days it was just turntables going through guitar amps, without even a PA system. Disco was on the radio, but Herc was playing James Brown, the Isley Brothers, and Aretha Franklin, and people responded. Eventually he and others started talking, or "rapping," over the records, just doing shout-outs and getting people dancing to the funk on the sound system. By 1975 Herc had started making real money at his DJ parties, charging a few dollars and packing in hundreds of people. By Bronx standards, he was sitting pretty, but nobody ever expected what he was doing to become a commercial force.

Afrika Bambaataa was known as an innovator, mixing any music with a beat into his DJ sets, combining funk with Bugs Bunny music, J. Geils Band, TV jingles, or the Rolling Stones. Like Herc, he promoted his own parties to give people a place to go and to spin interesting records. Break-dancers would show up and were sometimes featured on the bill.

Grandmaster Flash was an innovator who made rap music possible in the sense that he was the first to really extend the "get down part" of a song, as he called it, manipulating the spinning of the record to extend a few seconds to several minutes. He used his knowledge of electronics to "pre-hear" the record with head-phones, then use multiple turntables to keep repeating the same section of the song. Flash employed a young kid he knew who could really time the beats, "Grand Wizard Theodore," who put scratching into the mix as well. (Ironically, the first song he used as the scratch part in a performance was from the rock band Thin Lizzy.) When DJs started rapping over the scratch sounds and the beats, first rap, then what came to be hip-hop, was born.

A Tale of Technology on Two Coasts

Both early '80s rap scratching, which uses discs on turntables in front of a live audience, and today's hip-hop, with its sophisticated electronic studio mixes, depend heavily on technology. It's ironic then that while young NYC rap promoters were just beginning to feel the entrepreneurial urge, another group of would-be entrepreneurs on the West Coast were feeling the same urge, likewise brought on by new uses of technology. The East Coast guys were on the street hustling music in urban centers, but the West Coast boys, clustered mostly in California's Silicon Valley, were writing sophisticated business plans and hustling venture capitalists for huge sums of money.

The two groups were to chart very different paths into entre-preneurship. Each in their own way would come to typify a generation and one of the great periods of American economic growth. During the 1990s, with gangsta rap and hip-hop lyrics that disrespected women and much of the establishment, the rappers came to represent the underbelly of the country, while the establishment embraced the "Internet boys" as the saviors of the new economy. Neither proved to be the case.

Follow the Money

Business' number one lesson is "follow the money." The number two lesson: "Cash is king." Both groups, East Coast street hustlers and West Coast "Internet boys," knew the lessons well. The rappers followed their money from music to clothes to a host of other cultural products (jewelry, magazines, etc.) but always on the street. The Internet entrepreneurs beat a path to the cash on Sand Hill Road.

Sand Hill Road, in Menlo Park (just outside San Jose), is famous in investment circles as the home of America's best and brightest venture capitalists. Similar clusters of venture capitalists exist in many other parts of the country, like Boston or Austin, Texas, but California's Sand Hill Road is justifiably the most famous.

A venture capitalist operates like a bank, providing cash for promising start-up businesses, but instead of looking for a monthly repayment, takes part ownership in the new company. The venture capitalist looks to get his money back when the company is sold, merged, or goes public. Instead of deposits, venture capitalists raise money from rich individuals and institutions (in what are known as "funds") who want "professionals" to invest for them in new enterprises. Venture capitalists (sometimes called simply "VCs" but also often referred to as "vulture capitalists" by the founders who seek the money) review business plans from would-be entrepreneurs and decide what to finance. They extract a huge amount of equity (ownership) in return for their money.

Ripping the Hinges Off

The tradition before the Internet boom was that as much as 60 to 80 percent of the ownership of a new company would be given up for the cash needed to get started. By the time the mania of the Internet took hold, the whole equation was turned upside down. The hunted became the hunter. Like other "economic bubbles," a lot of it didn't make sense to outsiders, but eventually everybody wanted in. To raise millions, all you needed was a fancy dot-com name (sometimes the weirder the better) and a set of Microsoft PowerPoint charts that projected huge cash losses into the future, no real earnings, but the promise of everyone in the world eventually being connected to your Web site.

In his history of the time, *eBoys: The First Inside Account of Venture Capitalists at Work*, San Jose State University business historian Randall Stross describes how the Internet mania changed the world of the VC. He notes that one famous VC, Don Valentine, founder and head of Sequoia Capital, recognized amid the chaos of that time that the "professionals" had taken leave of their senses, raising money and indiscriminately flinging it at anything that came through the door. "I'm not sure what business I'm in," he said, "but we're in the venture capital business. We have billions when we used to have millions. We have limited partners ripping the hinges off the door to get into the next fund . . . Don't think for a moment that means we know what we're doing—we don't. The stock market in the 1990s has covered up our ineptitude."

Some of the mania, of course, resulted in real businesses that continue to grow and thrive today, including some of America's and the world's most successful and valuable: eBay, Google, Yahoo, Cisco, and Barry Diller's InterActive Corp. In addition, the Internet boys paved the way for old-line "bricks" businesses to add successful and profitable "clicks" to businesses such as WalMart.com and BestBuy.com. But at the end of the decade, the effort produced more losers than winners.

Most of these losing deals were private, and away from the prying eyes of the public. And not many people—investors in the funds, the VCs making the decisions, nor the Internet boys with the grand plans for world domination—want to publicly discuss what went wrong. Nor is that the purpose of this book. But the mistakes were legend and the losses astronomical. The accompanying chart (Losing Money by the Billions) provides just a brief look at a variety of the deals and the money that's gone forever.

Losing Money by the Billions

COMPANY	AMOUNT LOST?
save.com	$5m +
empori	$5m
ingredients.com	$5m
zap.com	$5.7m
hitplay media	$9m
headlight.com	$10m
bitlocker.com	$10m
zelerate	$10m
netmorf	$11m
zoza.com	$12m
foodline.com	$13m
zing.com	$14m
wwwrrr.com	$15m
eppraisals.com	$15m
myspace.com	$15m
epod.com	$18m
voter.com	$20m
hookt.com	$20m
send.com	$20m
ehobbies.com	$20m
onlinechoice.com	$20m + $10m debt
gtown.com	$22m
beautyjungle.com	$23m
promptu	$24m
ecircles.com	$24m
homebytes.com	$25m
Officeclick.com	$35m
urban box office	$35.5m
metalspectrum.com	$40m
carclub.com	$40m
freeride.com	$42m
multitude.com	$45m
dash.com	$50m

COMPANY	AMOUNT LOST?
zoho.com	$50m
iam.com	$50m
evoice.com	$51m
flooz.com	$51.5m
express.com	$55m
petopia.com	$66m
quepasa.com	$68m
wine.com	$70m
furniture.com	$75m
rivals.com	$75m
planetrx.com	$87.5
logictier	$90m
impresse	$90m
musicmaker.com	$117.6m
etoys.com	$200m
pets.com (& petstore.com)	$214.5m
cybergold.com	$225m + (estimated after several sales)
kozmo.com	$250m
broadband office	$250m
rx.com	$350m
go.com	$815m
questionexchange.com	$1b (combined with several others)
march first	$14b

(Source: *F'd Companies: Spectacular Dot-Com Flameouts* by Philip J. Kaplan, Simon & Schuster, April 2002)

Winners and Losers

To be sure, the VCs made mistakes, some big, some small. And while this book is about the hip-hop winners, the hip-hop community has also made its share of mistakes. Many have been referenced in parts of the book. But the difference is striking. This distinction is not pointed out to condemn the Internet investors, the entrepreneurs, or those who staked their lives and careers to follow a dream. Sometimes, however, the best way to see something more clearly is to look at what it's not, to find a contrast so sharp that it better illuminates the subject. And the sharpest contrast of all is how the hip-hop moguls followed the money and made cash the king.

Clearly the Internet mania is the analogue of the hip-hop craze. Both survived their early bouts with events that could have knocked them off course, and both have produced their share of winners and losers. Both, too, have their heroes and those they'd rather forget. And while the Internet bet its future on a technology that was alien to most users at the time, the hip-hop entrepreneurs lived the familiar, everyday life on the street.

Rappers Take on the World

In the early days, rap music was live music. Nobody really expected the sound to make its way to recordings. It's fitting, however, that the man who saw the recording potential, Russell Simmons, first saw it live. It was the live performance that transformed him, ultimately making him the first hip-hop mogul and one of the industry's leaders two decades later.

"Rapper's Delight" is usually cited as the record that set off the rap music phenomenon, and in a commercial sense it was. At one point the single was reportedly selling one hundred thousand copies a week in New York alone. The song was a huge success and it showed that the music had potential to bring in a lot of money. The Sugarhill Gang was not a real act, however, and was slapped together by its record company the same way many teen pop bands are today, with performers who weren't from the Bronx. As a result, many "real" rap performers resented the group, especially the Cold Crush Brothers, whose lyrics found their way into the song, without credit.

Russell Simmons did not have a hand in "Rapper's Delight," but he did have a hand in the first rap act to be signed to a major label: Kurtis Blow. Mercury Records picked up a single, "Christmas Rap," because the A&R person knew he could recoup the six-thousand-dollar cost in England alone. The single ended up selling around four hundred thousand copies. Simmons's first act also scored the first rap album to go gold, in 1980. But among Russell's firsts, he is the first to admit that he didn't do it alone.

Russell Reaches Out and Learns
Lesson Number One: Teamwork

No business today, Internet or hip-hop, can be built by one individual. Surrounding yourself with talent is a key to success. As Simmons notes in the last chapter ("Business and Life Lessons") of his biography, *Life and Def*, "You are only as good as the people around you. You can have a powerful vision, but without a staff that can make it happen, it's just a dream. I believe the most difficult thing in business is to find smart people and keep them."

One of those that Simmons reached out to early on was Lyor Cohen, an early promoter of rap acts who joined Simmons in 1983. Cohen has worked with Simmons almost from the very beginning. Simmons now considers him a partner and a friend. Although Cohen was a paid staffer at first, Simmons has given him increasing levels of responsibility and ownership. He is now one of the most prominent Jewish members of the hip-hop elite, but he's not the only one. In fact, several Jews operate in critical roles in the hip-hop infrastructure. (See "The Jews Behind Hip-Hop.")

Lesson Two: Service

If Simmons has learned the secret of success early, it is in his philosophy of service. It's what he tries to teach his interns and all those around him:

> Be of service and do something that will help people. My best interns have been people who were not just good leaders, but

The Jews Behind Hip-Hop

Historically, there has almost always been some level of animosity between the African American and the American Jewish communities. It was underscored when the Reverend Jesse Jackson, running for president, made some off-the-cuff remarks (that were within hearing of reporters) about the Jewish domination of New York City. Seldom do the two communities intersect. But when they do, they do so most noticeably in the entertainment business. Hip-hop is not an exception.

As reporter Matthew Cowan pointed out in his article "All About the Benjamins," in *Heeb* magazine, "Jewishness defies the hip-hop norm. Their presence on wax [the Beastie Boys and others] is nothing compared to what goes on behind the scenes. Indeed some of the biggest names in the business are Jewish: Lyor Cohen of Def Jam, Steve Rifkin of Loud Records, David Mays of *The Source*, to say nothing of those who course throughout the industry as label executives, entertainment lawyers, agents, publicists, producers, clothiers and jewelers."

Cowan argues that most stay well hidden behind the scenes, but goes on to name of few of the most visible:

Paul Rosenberg: Eminem's manager
Michael Selverine: entertainment attorney
Lee Resnick: Criminal Records
Larry Schwartz: CEO of Lugz
Larry Zimmer: president of Johnny Blaze clothing line
Marc Levin: film producer (Slam, Whiteboyz, Brooklyn Babylon)
Jonathon Wolfson: publicist for Suge Knight
Scott Storch: A-list music producer

While hip-hop enterprises are essentially black enterprises, there seems to be no animosity where business is concerned. Everyone—white, black, male, female—is part of the team. As Simmons says in his biography: "You must try to keep yourself open to people . . . Some companies believe that to be successful, everyone must fit a mold. If that were the case, I never would have made it out of Hollis."

good servants. They did their job so well that they made people depend on them. They provided a true service.

There's nothing I can tell you that hasn't been taught by someone else, especially by Mohammad, or Lord Buddha, or Abraham, or Jesus Christ. The basic principles have all been written. They're not going to change because one individual got creative. The more you serve, the happier you are. All the toys and junk we get come from being able to provide a service, to provide happiness. Service itself promotes happiness.

If we operate with service and harmony, we can be successful businesspeople. We can be real success stories when we are providing happiness. All of us want to be happy.

We can be real successful when we're making people happy. Everybody who sells everything is selling happiness. When consumers put their money down, the perception is that they are getting some form of happiness. In turn, you get back happiness. If what you are selling gives long-term happiness and has integrity, you will receive long-term happiness. Get up in the morning and say, "What can I give?" All of us have some kinds of gifts.

Ultimately, the gift that Russell gave the world was hip-hop itself.

Russell's Rap: A Gift to the World

In 1982 Grandmaster Flash and the Furious Five released "The Message," a watershed song that spoke of life on the streets in the big city. The song never made the pop charts, but it was a huge critical success and paved the way for rap's evolution from party music to social message music.

Russell Simmons was one of the few to see the full potential of rap music. A history of rap music in the 1980s is in large part a history of Russell Simmons's businesses. He fanatically believed it could cross over without having to be watered down. He stressed artistic integrity, but also pushed his artists to break boundaries. He started Def Jam with Rick Rubin in 1984 and signed future stars LL Cool J, the Beastie Boys, and Public Enemy.

The biggest payoffs came when black and white were jammed together in ways that nobody had seen before. Nobody took three white Jewish rappers seriously except Simmons and his partner Rick Rubin. Next thing you know, the album hit number one (the first rap album to do so), spawned a top-ten single, and sold five million copies. When Run-D.M.C. hooked up with Aerosmith to do a cover of "Walk This Way," it was another barrier-breaking smash. The song went to number six on the *Billboard* pop chart and the album, their third, sold three million copies.

Public Enemy's landmark albums of the late 1980s took social commentary to a new level, amplifying every protest song that had come out during the last two hundred years. The provocative titles of the second and third albums, *It Takes a Nation of Millions to Hold Us Back* and *Fear of a Black Planet,* gave an accurate picture of the lyrics and sonic cacophony contained.

The rest, as the saying goes, is history. Rap and later hip-hop, as it came to be called in the 1990s, set a steady pace up the charts. By the 2000s the genre was dominating the musical scene. Of course, not every aspect of hip-hop has been a success. Like every other form of entertainment, hip-hop has seen it all, from groundbreaking musical statements that didn't change the scene (such as A Tribe Called Quest or Lauren Hill) to massive commercial successes that turned out to be short-lived (such as Vanilla Ice or MC Hammer). "Urban music" now accounts for roughly a quarter of all CDs sold in the United States, the same proportion as rock. If you remove catalog titles from all genres, the percentage is even higher.

Besides their domination of the charts, the hip-hop impresarios have changed the music business in two fundamental ways. They got control over their own music and in so doing became exceedingly wealthy. And, not content to stay safely within the music industry as most had in the past, they used that money to create a large number of interlocking endeavors in a myriad of businesses. Many such as Diddy, Dash, Simmons, Carter, and Miller went on to found so many enterprises they've become what are known in business as "serial entrepreneurs." But it all started with money from the music.

As Craig Werner noted in the book *A Change Is Gonna Come: Music, Race, and the Soul of America*, "Becoming literate means learning to play the game by the real rules. You have to be smart enough to play the game within the game if you want to have any real chance of making it." With the exception of a few bad boys like Suge Knight, most of the rap music moguls have heeded Werner's key point: "The trick is to get paid without selling out your people."

And when it comes to getting paid, and not "not selling out his people," nobody does it better than Russell Simmons.

5

RUSSELL SIMMONS

Empires of the 'Hood

I cold chill at a party in a b-boy stance
And rock on the mic and make the girls wanna
    dance
Fly like a Dove, that come from up above
I'm rockin on the mic and you can call me Run-Love

—RUN-D.M.C.
"Sucker MCs," from the album *Run-D.M.C.*

MORE THAN ANY other hip-hop mogul, Russell Simmons, the original, has it all: leadership qualities . . . networking savvy . . . deal-making skills . . . and an intuitive feel for the changing pulse of the market.

High-profile CEOs rely heavily on these skills to capture and consolidate power at the top of today's massive *Fortune* 500 companies. The skills are often bred in their CEO bones by blue-blooded parents, then honed in the finest New England prep schools and polished to a fine point at Harvard or Wharton Business School. Most of today's big-name CEOs lead established, successful organizations begun decades ago by founders long since departed. Few of today's CEOs last more than five years in the top job. And the turnover rate is quickening each quarter.

Not so for Russell Simmons, the prototypical rap CEO. He is the man many credit with almost single-handedly creating the musical phenomena *and* blazing the road to riches for rap artists turned hip-hop business tycoons. He started the music label Def Jam in the 1980s with three thousand dollars. Now he's worth somewhere close to half a billion dollars. He's been at the top of his game for more than twenty-five years and has created a business empire that touches music, movies, fashion, wireless services, theater, jewelry, yoga, financial services, and more. *Inc.* magazine said, "Perhaps the most enduring legacy of Russell Simmons will be something he never set out to do. Simmons has emerged as an entrepreneurial role model, providing guidance both directly and indirectly."

Russell Simmons discovered and nurtured some of rap's earliest and most celebrated personalities, including Kurtis Blow, LL Cool J, the Beastie Boys, Slick Rick, Public Enemy, and of course, Run-D.M.C. The latter group's many firsts include being the first hip-hop artists to earn a platinum record, the first rap group on MTV, a multi-platinum record, and a *Rolling Stone* cover. The Beastie Boys were the first rap group to have a number one album on the *Billboard* sales chart.

But in the annals of big business success, Simmons is most noted for his contributions as an instinctive entrepreneur and innovative businessman. He pioneered the metamorphosis from rap impresario to well-connected business magnate and unparalleled urban lifestyle advocate. Along the way, he made himself one of the richest men in the world. Simmons paved the way for a whole generation of hip-hoppers to make the transition from rap music to Wall Street mogul. He single-handedly pioneered the development of "Empires of the 'Hood." His own, called Rush Communications, was the first, and to date, arguably the most successful.

As he told NPR's Terry Gross in a *Fresh Air* interview, black kids with not much education are earning serious money now just doing what they love and building a business. It's something that was not instilled in the black community before—to be an entrepreneurial businessman—and it is a change he is proud of.

● The Simmons File

1957   Born in Queens, New York. Second of three sons to Evelyn
and Daniel Simmons.

Older brother, Danny Simmons (cofounder of Def
Poetry Jam).

Younger brother, Reverend Joseph "Run" Simmons
(member of Run-D.M.C. and now president of Phat Farm
Footwear).

Grows up in a middle-class family in Hollis, Queens.
Sells drugs on the street to buy clothes; graduates high
school.

1977   Drops out of City College of New York just before
graduation.

1977   Begins business career as concert promoter, producer, and
manager of hip-hop groups.

1979   Releases first record, by Kurtis Blow.

1982   Gets first big break managing group Run-D.M.C., which
includes brother Reverend Run. Debut album goes gold.
Eventually promotes crossover tie-in with Aerosmith in
1986. Recognizes the value of street culture and lifestyle
and arranges multimillion-dollar deal for Run-D.M.C. with
Adidas.

1985   With Rick Rubin, forms Def Jam Records, which eventually
features Slick Rick, Whodini, Public Enemy, Beastie Boys,
and LL Cool J, among others. Gets $600,000 from Sony for
production deal.

1990   Founds Rush Communications holding company.

1992   Launches Def Comedy Jam on HBO.

1994–96   Sells 60 percent of his share of Def Jam Records to Polygram for an undisclosed sum to gain better distribution.

1999   Sells his remaining share of Def Jam Records to Universal
Music (which had merged with Polygram) for $120 million
but remains chairman.

2001 Launches Def Poetry Jam on HBO with brother Danny. Broadway show version and touring shows follow. Production wins a Peabody Award and Tony Award.

2003 Sells Phat Fashions, its licensing organization, and main trademarks, Baby Phat and Phat Farm, to Kellwood LLC for a total of $140 million. Agreement leaves him running the company and his wife serving as designer for her lines.

2003 Launches prepaid Visa RushCard with Unifund Corporation and distributes 500,000 cards in the first eighteen months.

2003 *Fast Company* magazine labels Simmons "arguably, the most creative, successful, and respected African-American entrepreneur."

2003 Publicly battles with Pepsi over double standards in endorsements and wins an agreement from them to avoid a national boycott.

2004 Forms Simmons Jewelry partnership with M. Fabrikant & Sons jewelry distributors to market a line of Phat Farm jewelry.

2004 Launches Def Filmmakers film production and distribution.

2004 Named one of twenty-seven "Men of the Year" in *GQ* magazine.

2005 Launches Russell Simmons Music Group with old label Def Jam.

2005 Launches yoga DVD line with Good Times Entertainment.

Instead of just rapping about what a great MC they are, "Rappers rap now about being CEOs. Some of them rap more about how they can stack money and how they do it," he says. "They rap about how they run their businesses."

Simmons didn't pick up his business acumen from Harvard Business School. He did attend City College of New York, but, like Bill Gates and Michael Dell, he dropped out of college before graduating. Instead, he learned his CEO skills on the mean streets of Queens, New York.

Unlike many of the rapper-businessmen who came after him, however, it can't be said that Simmons came from an impoverished background. Both his parents were college grads working at professional jobs. But his early business experience didn't come from genes bequeathed by his parents or from lofty discussions around the dinner table. Simmons learned his first CEO skills—leadership and understanding cash management—by selling fake drugs on the street. (It was legal, he says, and had much better profits than illegal drugs.) He learned fast running with a gang known as the "Seven Immortals." As he told NPR's *Fresh Air,* "It inspired me to buy for one, sell for two."

Starting in the mid '80s promoting the first New York rappers, he took a just-emerging Harlem sound and successfully marketed it to urban and suburban masses around the globe via his label, Def Jam Records, and Rush Communications (named after one of his most telling nicknames, Rush). Rush Communications eventually became the overall business vehicle for his varied empire. Today he runs a long list of successful ventures, and his number is on the cell phone presets of dozens of people in power, from Donald Trump to Hillary Clinton to *Fortune* 100 CEOs.

How he got to his exalted position is no secret for those who are willing to carefully study the rise of Russell Simmons from street hustler to Wall Street mogul. *His skills?* The same as every successful *Fortune* 500 CEO. *His secret?* Imprinting his own style on those skills then pushing them to the max. For Simmons, the secrets of his multimillion-dollar success lie in his leadership focus, his partnering skills, his capacity to truly empower those around him, his knack of sensing social-cultural trends, and his uncanny ability to build and leverage enduring consumer brands.

Leadership

Simmons is a true leader, not a manager. There is a difference and it's an important one.

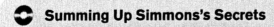 **Summing Up Simmons's Secrets**

I. **Leadership:** *not* management!

Vision: *Keep the big picture in mind by keeping your eyes on the horizon.*

Persistence: *When you believe you're right, wait till the world comes to you.*

Integrity: *Doing what you'll say you'll do.*

Empathy: *Remembering where you're from, and giving back.*

Authenticity: *Understanding what unites rather than divides.*

II. **Partnering:** to fill the voids and complete the customer value proposition.

III. **Empowerment:** surrounding himself with smart people and letting them do their thing.

IV. **Sensing Trends:** tuning in to what's happening around him and understanding what's important and lasting.

V. **Building and Leveraging Brands:** recognizing the power of music at the center of the urban culture and building and leveraging lifestyle brands into almost every facet of life.

Simmons is about business, not management. And business is about *leadership.* For all the media attention on his political activism and jet-set lifestyle, Simmons takes care of business, and leadership comes first.

Management is about plotting the minutiae, controlling the action, organizing the workflow, sweating the details, and recording the results. Leadership is about understanding the big trends, catching the wave, understanding the next big move, motivating people smarter than you to do great things for you, leading from the front of the crowd to places they've never been before.

Management is about time: understanding it, measuring it, allocating, monitoring, and controlling it. And since time is money, management is about ensuring that money earned is in a profitable proportion to time spent. Leadership is about space:

knowing where, when, how, and most importantly why, and where (what business leaders call "space") people are going to spend their money.

Management is about taking orders from above and then not messing them up when passing them along to those below. Leadership is about knowing the orders to give.

Management is about following the crowd to ensure that you pick up your fair share of what they leave behind. Leadership is about leading the crowd to places it never knew it could go. When Simmons launched an urban clothing line, few of his peers took it seriously, he says. "All the rappers laughed at me then, and now they all have their own lines coming out."

Management is about minimizing risk and earning a salary. Leadership is about taking calculated risks and reaping big, big rewards. It's about creating wealth and sustainable enterprises that manage themselves even while you sleep. It's about dreaming big and living large.

Perhaps Simmons's greatest success secret is giving his full attention first to leadership, and then thinking about management. By observing how Simmons created and runs his empire, it appears that for him, leadership means five things: vision, persistence, integrity, empathy, and a focus on the authentic, universal truths that make people around the world the same, not different.

VISION

Management of a business is about allocating its time and money and then closely watching the details of how the organization operates. Leadership of a business is identifying where that "somewhere" is. It's called vision.

Vision is a mysterious thing. Some people have a natural ability to see things how they might be, not just the way they are. Often the ability to "envision" is innate, a consequence of a natural curiosity about life, and an inbred, relentless desire to know about things just beyond current horizons.

Being born a visionary is a true gift. But staying a visionary is a matter of routine. The world's great visionaries—like Gates and Simmons—work hard at polishing their gift. For them it's become an instinctive habit, and that habit can be learned. It starts with curiosity and keeping yourself open to new ideas. Curiosity is something we're all born with, but somehow most of us lose it along the way. Simmons is certainly curious. He has become adept at keeping himself open to new ideas, new trends, and new ways of doing things. His favorite, most consistent question, particularly when completing a deal or finishing a project: "What else?"

Simmons is always on the lookout for the next big thing and usually finds it before anyone else notices the obvious. He was the first to see that rap music was a lifestyle and could be translated into clothes, shoes, beverage, entertainment, design, watches, cars, and even financial services. He was the first to see that the wave of black, hip, urban chic could create a whole new market for cultural products that would transcend its inner-city New York neighborhoods and become an image emulated around the globe.

Simmons knows, too, that not every great vision comes fully formed, neatly wrapped, fully guaranteed, and ready to use. While most often on the money, he's not always right. His idea for a marketing consulting firm, to help traditional marketers tap into the hip-hop movement, called dRush (with partner Deutsch Inc., a preeminent New York advertising firm), didn't work. He closed it after it didn't catch on the way he envisioned. His magazine venture, *One World*, faded away quietly after failing to make a steady profit.

Simmons knows when to "fold 'em." But he also knows when to "hold 'em."

PERSISTENCE

Simmons knows that the second great secret of leadership is persistence. When the ideas are right, when you feel it in the bones, you dig your heels in and wait for the world to come to you. Confident in his convictions, Simmons hangs in until the vision becomes a reality. The mark of a true entrepreneur is not getting an idea and starting a business, it's taking an idea and sticking with it. "Being an entrepreneur is having a little faith and confidence and not quitting," he says.

As his friend Donald Trump says about Simmons, "I consider him one of the great entrepreneurs out there today. He's a fabulous guy with a tremendous understanding of business." And the role model of a persistent entrepreneur is what captured the attention of *Entrepreneur* magazine as well. They dubbed it the "Russell Effect" for his ability to perceptively and patiently take his successful formula in music and apply it to businesses that have little in common with music.

Clearly, Simmons knows his own mind and has developed an uncanny ability to recognize value and wait for it to come to him. The quiet confidence he has developed over the years has much to do with his almost unbroken string of successes. As one business associate has said, "nearly everything he touches turns to gold."

But turning ideas into gold requires a special touch. Usually that means strength of character to withstand the inevitable ups and downs of business. For Simmons, that comes in large part through his devotion to yoga, something he practices everyday without fail. His daily visits to Jivamukti (an upscale yoga spa with a distinct spiritual philosophy) help him focus both his body and his mind. It keeps him centered on what's important, like persistence in getting to what he knows is right, and integrity in doing so.

INTEGRITY

Integrity plays a strong role in how Simmons leads his company and how he develops the next generation of leaders.

Warren Buffett is the most important business leader (not business manager) in the modern history of the United States. He's made more money than anyone ever, except Bill Gates. Buffett's secret is outstanding leadership, not management (he doesn't manage much of anything except money), and his approach is simple: find the right business, put the right people in place to run them, then leave them alone to do their job.

In large part, then, Simmons's success is absolutely dependent on his ability to recognize and employ true business leaders to run his companies. His formula? Again, it's pretty simple: "In evaluating people you look for three things: integrity, intelligence, and energy. But if you don't have the first, the other two will kill you."

Simmons has nothing if not integrity. What he says doesn't always please the establishment, but he is absolutely consistent in his thoughts, words, and actions. Partners and business associates say you can take his word to the bank, often with just a handshake. Those who are close to him have been with him for years.

For Simmons, integrity means not just saying, but doing. "If we operate with service and harmony, we can be successful business people," he says. "We can be real success stories when we are providing happiness." Integrity also applies to what he sells. "Keep integrity in your product" is one of his mantras.

At the same time, Simmons always keeps one foot on the street and never hesitates to use his money and influence to help the urban community. But Simmons doesn't believe in charity for charity's sake. He believes that success breeds success and that young black men and women need to make money themselves so they can give back to the community.

EMPATHY

Some people, when they achieve riches, fame, and power, lose sight of where they came from and how they got to where they are now. They are afraid to tell it like it is, because they don't want to upset their newly acquired friends or undermine their newly acquired status in polite society. Not Simmons.

Simmons has stayed true to his roots. He talks openly about what he thinks is wrong and about how to make it right. More importantly, he gives back to the community. As he says, he wants "to contribute more to earth than I take away from it." "When you get up in the morning you should think, 'What can I give?' not 'What can I get?'" he says.

The examples of Simmons giving back abound:

○ The Hip-Hop Summit Action Network, is a nonprofit, nonpartisan coalition of hip-hop artists, entertainment industry leaders, education advocates, civil rights proponents, and youth leaders. They are united in the belief that hip-hop is an enormously influential agent for social change, which must be utilized to fight the war on poverty and injustice. Started and largely supported by Simmons, the group stages youth conferences around the country. Its aim in the last presidential election was to increase voter registration by twenty million. Simmons's disciples and friends set up gatherings—part rally, part concert—to get out the vote. Will Smith, LL Cool J, Beyonce, Puff Daddy, Ice Cube, Snoop Dogg, and others hosted their own rallies. Local mayors often pitched in to help.

○ In partnership with Chrysler, the Hip-Hop Summit Action Network stages "Get Your Money Right" events throughout the country, bringing forth a message of financial empowerment for eighteen- to thirty-five-year-olds. The all-day events cover financial literacy, money management, and entrepreneurship.

○ The Rush Communications Philanthropic Arts Network, formed in 1995 by Russell and his brothers, Danny and Joseph, is aimed at gaining greater access to the arts for disadvantaged youth. The organization reportedly gives away some $350,000 per year to groups that introduce the arts to underprivileged kids.

○ A part of the profits from his new financial services debit card and from his energy drink, DefCon3, go to fund the Rush Communications organizations described above and Simmons's related philanthropic interests.

Simmons says he will never run for political office, but he has been an outspoken part of the political process. He speaks out on issues and tirelessly works on getting help for urban community problems. As he told *Index* magazine, "We're going through a tough period in America, and they can't afford to raise the minimum wage? I'm an American and I can afford not to get a tax break. I've got a thirty-thousand-square-foot house, what do I need a tax break for?"

Simmons told *USA Today* that he cared little about money. He makes it, he said, so he can give it away. Simmons went on to say that although he'll probably be remembered as a leader of hip-hop, he would rather be remembered as a philanthropist. "When I die, I hope they put that on my tombstone. 'You've got to make a lot of money to give away a lot of money.'"

He recognizes that his mission (putting more into life than you take out) is a hollow dream if you don't have margin (something to put back).

AUTHENTIC, UNIVERSAL TRUTHS

Many traditional American businesses grew increasingly international in their market outlook in the late '60s and '70s, an interest largely forced upon them by the aggressive new competition from Europe and Japan. As American businesses began to "fight back," investing huge sums to actively market their products abroad, courses in international marketing became the rage in U.S. business schools. Such courses stressed understanding the differences between the U.S. consumer market and foreign markets.

Once these newly minted MBAs hit the streets for their U.S. companies, they poured billions into ferreting out the minutest nuances of differences between their American customers and those in other countries. When that didn't work quite as well as they hoped, they came to realize that the real secret of success was understanding the global, universal truth: people around the world have more in common than they have differences.

Before they spent all that time and money, they could have asked Russell Simmons. He knew from the beginning, he knew from the street, he knew from understanding rather than judging people, that the gold was in the similarities not the differences. And he built his Empire of the 'Hood on that conviction.

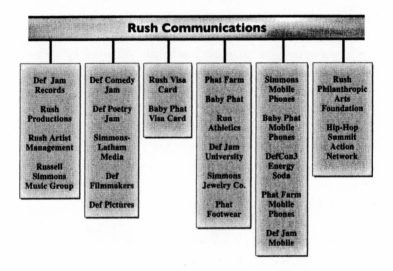

Rush Communications					
Def Jam Records	**Def Comedy Jam**	**Rush Visa Card**	**Phat Farm**	**Simmons Mobile Phones**	**Rush Philanthropic Arts Foundation**
Rush Productions	**Def Poetry Jam**	**Baby Phat Visa Card**	**Baby Phat**	**Baby Phat Mobile Phones**	**Hip-Hop Summit Action Network**
Rush Artist Management	**Simmons-Latham Media**		**Run Athletics**	**DefCon3 Energy Soda**	
Russell Simmons Music Group	**Def Filmmakers**		**Def Jam University**	**Phat Farm Mobile Phones**	
	Def Pictures		**Simmons Jewelry Co.**	**Def Jam Mobile**	
			Phat Footwear		

Simmons's approach is always to focus first on the truth about his core market (he likes to say that they can smell the truth) and then extend it to the world. Getting to the truth means always being "authentic," another favorite in Simmons's leadership vocabulary. Authenticity in one market leads to authenticity elsewhere.

Simmons's focus on the truth, the authentic, is eerily reminiscent of another great leader, Winston Churchill, who said: "The truth is incontrovertible. Malice may attack it, ignorance may deride it, but in the end, there it is." Churchill used the truth to save an empire; Simmons is using it to create one. Focus on the authentic universal truths about people: vision, empathy, a desire to "give back," and perhaps most important of all, persistence, is at the core of Simmons's leadership style.

Partnering

It is almost impossible today for any company to succeed on its own. Everyone needs partners, or more precisely, a network of partners, in order to successfully meet the tough demands of today's media-savvy consumers. Sometimes those partners supply ideas, while others supply money, manufacturing infrastructure, marketing smarts, or distribution systems.

Simmons was developing his partnering skills long before most business schools put it on their required reading list. "The way to get that paper is to help somebody else get that paper," Simmons is fond of saying. His first major partnership was an unlikely one, with white record producer Rick Rubin. Together they formed Def Jam Records, a company that made both men very wealthy and produced a long list of platinum albums. Most tellingly, several of the acts they signed in the mid '80s are still successful today, including LL Cool J and the Beastie Boys.

Simmons partnered with a major label distributor (Columbia/CBS) as soon as he had the leverage to strike a deal. When that relationship became strained, he sold part of his stake to Polygram in order to regain priority status within a distribution company. Along the way, he has had one criterion for partners: an equal drive to succeed. "It's important that every company I partner with is run by somebody who works as hard as me," he says.

Over the years, he built strong relationships with HBO, film producers, and clothing retailers. He and clothing distributor Kellwood partnered in a trial run with the Def Jam University line. Once both were comfortable with the relationship, they struck a lasting deal: Simmons sold his Phat Farm clothing brands for a cool $140 million.

His partnership with HBO, now in its second decade, has helped both parties reach a wider audience. Def Comedy Jam drew a whole new viewership to the channel, while the show allowed comics to reach a far bigger audience than usual. It helped turbo-charge the careers of acts such as Martin Lawrence, Chris Rock,

Bernie Mac, and Cedric the Entertainer. Simmons has extended that partnership with the Def Poetry show, an implausible concept that the two partners have turned into a success. The show won a Peabody Award and is now in its fifth season. It seems that there's a new deal announced almost daily. As this book was being written, he and his wife, Kimora Lee Simmons, formed the Simmons Jewelry company with M. Fabrikant & Sons, one of the world's largest distributors of polished diamonds and jewelry. He also formed a design partnership with Griamaldi and a cell phone deal with Motorola, launched a yoga video line and a wireless phone service, and got called back in by Def Jam to form Russell Simmons Music Group.

The line to partner with Simmons is a long one. Partners are attracted no doubt by his unequalled success, but also by his growing reputation to be a true believer in empowerment—letting people have the freedom to do what they do best.

Empowerment

In all respects Simmons is a leader, not a follower; a businessman, not a manager. He's a delegator, not a doer. When talking about his sprawling empire, he says, "Every company is run by someone smarter than me." He delegates most everything but the essential tasks, such as making critical design decisions in his clothing line and prospecting for new business opportunities to those around him. Never the master of detail, nor wanting to be, Simmons focuses on leadership—from the front, not the back—and wastes little time worrying about yesterday, just tomorrow.

Importantly, Simmons recognized early that he couldn't get where he wanted to go all by himself. And where he wanted to go was no less than to take the hip urban lifestyle to mainstream America and eventually to the world. That's quite a trip from Queens, even for someone who dreams as big as Simmons. Simmons realized that he'd need help, and he wasn't afraid or too egotistical to get it. To his credit, from the beginning to the present, he's instinctively sought out others to help him make his dream a reality.

When his wife, Kimora, a former runway model, made some critical remarks about his women's clothing line prototypes, he reportedly said, "Well, take care of it." And she did, taking over the creative team and altering designs to make them more appealing. The line quickly grew to over $35 million in annual sales.

In 1998 he approached Ruby Azrak, a New York–based clothing executive Simmons knew from fashion shows, for advice on how to run Phat Farm. After Azrak made some suggestions, the two signed a $75 million licensing deal with a handshake and the apparel business exploded.

Simmons knows that through empowerment, his organization can scale up and thrive. "The president of a company also has to be a good servant," he says. "He has to provide a service to his people to make them feel good about what they're doing. You become a great leader by being a great servant. There's not much difference in that sense between being an intern and being the top leader."

Sensing Trends

Most celebrated business leaders like to talk about having a *feel* for the market. They think having the feel is a gift that sets them apart from mere run-of-the-mill, pencil-pushing administrators who care-take existing businesses. The feel is a tingle in the bones that comes from sensing, understanding, knowing there's a new trend around before anyone else. And once you've got that feeling, the strategy is to exploit the trend as quickly as possible.

A fast-to-market strategy that the business hotshots often like to use is the "brand extension." A brand extension means taking a successful brand name from one product category, liquor for example, and extending it to another, and often close product category, such as beer. Why? Because it costs a lot of money to create awareness and loyalty for a new brand. So, the thinking goes, you "borrow" that awareness and loyalty and apply it to the new product. And, in theory, the result will be a big, quick success.

But, like the sexy sirens on the rocks who lured sailors to their death, brand extensions can be a path to a business shipwreck. Often they end up being clumsy attempts that fall flat. Many of the elite companies that have consistently pulled it off—including Virgin, Sony, Microsoft, Samsung, and Procter & Gamble—have put millions of shareholder dollars into creating a market for each brand extension. Unfortunately, even with close categories like beer and liquor it generally doesn't work; business history is full of just such flops. Now, try to extend the category even further from the liquor brand, say to a perfume, and you'll generally get a colossal failure, with the perfume product being dead in the water and potentially even damaging the original liquor brand in the process.

Like his big business brethren, Simmons clearly has a feel for the market. But he also touches, tastes, hears, and sees market potential where others are deaf, dumb, and blind. He seems to posses an all-senses approach that has allowed him to defy the conventional wisdom where most brand extensions fail, and fail big. Rather than creating a "push" extension, Simmons launches brand extensions that are created by demand—even if it is a demand that only he sees coming. Only a handful of trend-sensing marketing elite have managed to make that transition. Like Simmons, they tend to be rebels like Virgin's Richard Branson or EasyJet and EasyCruise founder Stelios Haji-Ioannou.

Simmons sees a market coming and quickly co-opts it, often with little or no money of his own at stake. He realized early on that hip-hop was part of a lifestyle, not just a form of music. He saw the potential to bring that lifestyle, and the desire to be a part of it, to a mass audience. He has the unique knack to focus on the core market, then drive it to the mainstream. Most importantly, Simmons sees lifestyle products as ingredients in one big trend stew, not as isolated product lines. Why can't clothing, watches, credit cards, cars, and a cell phone all share a similar brand name? Apart from Branson, no one had ever thought about brand extending quite like this before, much less made it work. But Simmons has, because he has an intuitive trend-sensing ability that tells him where to go and how far to push it. He has repeatedly caught the wave and rode it across multiple lines of business. In fact, Simmons has created one of the biggest brand extensions of all time, taking the hip-hop lifestyle from Harlem and extending it to the world. And he did it with a simple premise: focus on a core niche market, then drive it to the mainstream.

Some "preppy white" clothing brands, such as Polo, Tommy Hilfiger, and Timberland, caught on with urban youth almost by accident. Simmons was able to take that trend in the other direction, seeing what the hip-hop crowd wanted and knowing it would spread to the mainstream a few months to a year later.

It's one thing to sense a market trend and create a suite of brands to serve it, but it's quite another to keep it going strong for any sustained period of time. Here again, Simmons comes up big. He not only sensed the potential and built the products and brands to meet the market needs, but he's kept it going for more than two decades.

Building Enduring Brands

In the ephemeral, hit-driven music business, there are very few artists who endure. However, many of Simmons's early signings are still relevant and successful today. LL Cool J still cranks out the hits and sells millions, in addition to being a successful actor. The Beastie Boys have remained credible, respected, and popular after being written off as a faddish joke at the time of their first release. Simmons built up the Def Jam brand so high that he was able to sell it for $100 million.

There have been missteps and down years along the way, but the Def Jam label still commands respect twenty years later and has been extended to include Def Jam South. It's almost a sure bet that people will still be buying and talking about Def Jam's artists—including originals such as Public Enemy and Run-D.M.C.—a decade from now.

It would be easy to dismiss Simmons's foray into clothing lines if it had just flared up and then flared out. But Simmons saw the trends, moved as they moved, and always stayed on top of what was coming next. St. Louis–based Kellwood is known as a conservative apparel company, but they struck a nine-figure deal with Simmons and put the clothes into department stores. Phat Farm, Baby Phat, and Def Jam University are now mainstream brands that retailers can't ignore.

Def Comedy Jam ran for a decade on HBO, an enviable run for any television show, much less one that was considered a huge gamble at its launch. Def Poetry Jam was also considered a long shot. It has created its own legacy, with five seasons on HBO and a stage show both on tour and on Broadway. The addition of the

◓ The Simmons Brands

Baby Phat

DefCon3

Def Jam Comedy Festival

Def Jam Mobile

Def Jam Records

Def Jam Poetry Jam

Def Jam University

Phat Farm

Phat Footwear

Run Athletics

RushCard Visa

Rush Artist Management

Rush Productions

Russell Simmons Music Group

Simmons-Latham Media

Simmons Jewelry

RushCard prepaid Visa/debit card has been another unqualified success.

Marketing executives say the hip-hop power on mainstream culture is here to stay. Some estimate that hip-hop influences about one-quarter of all discretionary spending in this country. Russell Simmons and the Empire of the 'Hood, which he created from scratch and built into a worldwide phenomenon, is clearly the catalyst of that new market.

The Simmons name has become a brand in itself, enough that his new music label is called Russell Simmons Music Group. As Shawn "Jay-Z" Carter said when the label was announced, "History has yet to catch up with the greatness of Russell Simmons and the extent of his contributions to our music and culture. It is impossible to imagine the state of hip-hop today without accounting for Russell's visionary leadership over the past twenty years."

So maybe it's time they started studying Russell Simmons at the Harvard Business School!

6

FROM THE BELLY OF THE BEAST

Gangsta Rap Roots;
Hip-Hop's Cultural Myth

All we know is violence, do tha job in silence
Walk tha city streets like a rat pack of tyrants

—TUPAC SHAKUR
"Trapped," from the album *2Pacalypse Now*

From Cop Killer to *Law & Order*

African American actor Tracy Marrow stars as an important member of a small group of tough but sympathetically portrayed police detectives in one of the country's most popular shows, *Law & Order: Special Victims Unit*. At a time when TV schedules are crammed full of "realistic" cop shows, *Law & Order: SVU* is one of the most popular. The cops on the show are sensitive to the cultural crosscurrents of their community (Manhattan), and are depicted as real heroes defending the "special victims" of particularly heinous crimes. The cops come across as real people with real emotions and as great role models.

Its ironic, then, that Marrow, more popularly known as Ice-T, is the rapper who almost single-handedly touched off the gangsta rap genre with the 1986 song "6 'n the Morning." The song and Ice-T were major influences on the gangsta rap music that was to come. He created a huge national controversy in 1991 when his rap/rock hybrid band, Body Count, released the song "Cop

Killer." Marrow answered his critics by saying that, as Ice-T, he was singing as a character, and that "if you believe that I'm a cop killer, you believe David Bowie is an astronaut."

Ice-T wasn't the only singing (pseudo) cop killer out there though. As the 1980s came to a close, a South Central Los Angeles group called N.W.A. (Niggaz With Attitude) accelerated the anti-establishment, anti-cop rhetoric. The proudly confrontational group included Ice-T's almost namesake, Ice Cube, who was the band's founder. He was joined by Dr. Dre, MC Ren, and Eazy-E. In 1989 they released the album *Straight Outta Compton* on Eazy-E's Ruthless Records. This polarizing and controversial record became the first gangsta rap album to find a mass audience, seriously shocking millions across the country.

If the hip-hop story of entrepreneurial success has a dark side—as many, if not all businesses do—then it is this particular part of rap that is glorifying violence, celebrating thuggery, and, through lyrics and videos, portraying women as little more than sex objects or property to be bought and sold. Nowhere is this more evident than in that slice of rap known as "gangsta rap." While elements of this approach still permeate the music of artists such as Snoop Doggy and 50 Cent, the cop killer element has largely disappeared.

Rap: Not the First, Not the Last

Virtually every industry has a dark side. Hip-hop is no different. Money has often been made and businesses started to the accompaniment of illicit sex, gratuitous violence, and other forms illegal activity. The hip-hop business, of course, isn't the first to rise to legitimacy from less than savory roots. Whether the men who built America's infrastructure and foundation were "captains of industry" or "robber barons" is often in the eye of the beholder:

- ✪ John D. Rockefeller (after whom Damon Dash and Jay-Z named their Roc-A-Fella Records) was richer in today's dollars than

Bill Gates, and he got that way partly by bribing politicians and secretly buying up rivals.

● Andrew Carnegie's steel mills forced men to work twelve-hour days, seven days a week.

● In the 1860s Jay Gould sold $5 million in fraudulent stock and continually manipulated the markets for his own gain.

● The Seagram Company Ltd., of entertainment mogul Edgar Bronfman Jr., created its original fortune running rum into the United States from Canada during Prohibition.

● In the 1960s and '70s, Bernie Cornfeld and Robert Vesco, who through their Investors Overseas Service company bilked some $2 billion from investors, personified corporate malfeasance of the period, leading Congress in the early 1980s to press for (but never pass) several pieces of legislation to limit financial excesses.

● Junk bonds dominated the financial headlines during the 1980s, and nobody did it better than Michael Milken, dubbed "The Junk Bond King" on Wall Street. The king, however, didn't sit on his throne too long. He was prosecuted for racketeering and fraud by a then largely unknown U.S. attorney general, Rudy Giuliani, and served twenty-two months in jail, paid fines of more than $250 million and restitution to others of some $400 million.

● Ah, and then there were the go-go '90s, when corporate and banking greed and excesses were glorified in books and later in movies such as *Wall Street*, *Barbarians at the Gate*, and *The Smartest Guys in the Room*.

● The U. S. Securities and Exchange Commission, which was created as a reaction to the stock fraud and manipulation that was rampant in the 1930s, became the lead player in the corporate controversies that erupted in the '90s. They removed the veneer that had sugarcoated many financial reports to investors.

The fallout from the '90s is still front-page news a decade later as the criminal and civil cases slowly wind their way through the judicial labyrinth. The litigants are companies that were at the pinnacle of corporate America in the 1990s, now humbled in light of stock fraud, earnings manipulation, and tax evasion. Among those that went under the microscopes of federal and state authorities were the former and current cream of American business: Merrill Lynch, WorldCom, RiteAid, Enron, Tyco, Adelphia, Vivendi Universal, Nortel Networks, Lucent, AIG Insurance, Global Crossing, Edison Schools, Citigroup, Merck, Xerox, Quest Communications, CMS Energy, ImClone, JP Morgan Chase, and EDS, to name only a handful.

While rap was ripping up the turf between LA and New York City in the mid to late '90s, the pages of the *Wall Street Journal* were filled to capacity with investigative stories about companies that we now know were cooking the books and ripping off shareholders. Thousands of jobs were lost. Billions of dollars in equity, including many employees' life savings, disappeared. And some of the most admired names in established and entrepreneurial business have been indicted and either are serving time or under investigation: Kenneth Lay, Martha Stewart, Dennis Kozlowski, Richard Scrushy, and Bernie Ebbers, with many more to come.

Gangsta Rap: No Worse, No Betta

As everyone with a mother knows, the excuse that "everyone's doing it" doesn't go very far. But, like the rest of American business that found itself in trouble, gangsta rap has its apologists and detractors. And, again like the corporate messes of the 1990s, everyone has a theory of what went wrong and why.

Some critics have made a case against gangsta rap and the still frequent antisocial nature of the lyrics—simply as an aberration in American society (although there is no arguing about the deaths of Tupac Shukar or Biggie Smalls, along with nine others associated with them). Some others have argued that gangsta rap was an "authentic" reflection of life in the streets. And still others, that it was a "necessary evil" in the development of the genre.

Regardless of the perspective taken, gangsta rap and even its less graphic and violent hip-hop derivatives may well be the very foundation for the worldwide popularity of hip-hop. What can't be argued is the fact that hip-hop has found an audience and struck a chord among billions of people worldwide. Hip-hop music, lifestyle, products, and performance have become a "cultural brand," deeply embedded in the American and global psyche of a generation. Hip-hop, and in particular the stars and entrepreneurs who personify it, have become icons that are truly "above the rim."

Hip-Hop Playas: Brand Icons

In his seminal book on branding, *How Brands Become Icons: The Principles of Cultural Branding,* Harvard Business School professor Douglas B. Holt describes what he calls "cultural icons": "a person or thing regarded as a *representative symbol,* especially of a culture or a movement; a person or an institution considered worthy of admiration or respect." Few brands reach such status, he argues, because only a few brands have what it takes to spin "such compelling myths that they have become icons." His research has illuminated the entire new discipline of understanding the power and development of brands called "cultural branding."

Brand icons rise above the "massive cultural content" in markets crowded with information, products, and brands. These superior brand icons create market shares far beyond their competitors, because consumers come to value and buy the products "as much for what they symbolize as what they do . . . Consumers flock to brands that embody the ideals they admire, brands that express who they want to be."

Nowhere is cultural branding more evident than in "consumer high-involvement products used as a means of self expression, such as clothing, home décor." Cultural branding can be applied to cultural products or to individuals such as entertainment and sports stars.

Hip-Hop: Identity Myth Extraordinaire

Iconic brands can't be created for just any product or personality, however. Holt goes on to describe several necessary ingredients for the development of brand icons. To be successful, he says, they must (among other things):

- address acute cultural contradictions in society,
- perform identity myths that address these desires and anxieties,
- have identity myths that reside in the brand that consumers experience and share via ritual action,
- be set in populist worlds, and
- perform as activists, leading culture.

It seems the script on cultural branding was written especially for hip-hop. Holt goes on to point out another advantage that, when applied to hip-hop, completes the story: *icon brands enjoy a halo effect.* In other words, if the iconic brand truly fills a need for consumers, they ascribe to it much greater value and forgive much that would negate the brand.

One of the most critical aspects of cultural branding—the *identity myth*—helps explain, at least in part, the transforming power of hip-hop as it moved out of the ghetto and into the suburbs. Strong identity myths reside in certain products, or have been embedded in those products by masterful marketing and product positioning. Examples include Mountain Dew (the "slacker" myth), Marlboro (the Western frontier myth), Harley-Davidson (man-of-action myth), and, from an earlier era, Volkswagen (the Bohemian myth).

While Holt's analysis didn't extend to hip-hop, the genre seems to have written the script for a cultural branding megahit, and the brands themselves—Phat Farm, Sean John, Diddy, and Jay-Z—are already on their way to icon status. While there is an argument to be made for the negative impact of gangsta rap, there is an equal and more persuasive argument to the contrary: gangsta rap set in motion the precise and powerful "acute cultural contradiction" (the emasculated urbanite, struggling against the controlling elite—the cops, big business, government).

Gangsta: Cultural Contradiction

If hip-hop has a myth, it is surely the poor street hustler making good and living a platinum lifestyle. An essential ingredient in this idea of the street hustler—the thug, the gangsta—is rooted not in the "softer" hip-hop of today, but as a direct result of the power of gangsta rap. Contrary to what many would like to believe, West Coast gangsta rap created the hard edge for East Coast hip-hop. The gangstas demanded a response from the East Coast rappers, and they responded in kind. Whether it was staged or not (as some have argued), the myth of hip-hop as representative of life just outside the rules was indelibly written on the American psyche. It was embraced by all those who didn't really want to break the law, but wanted to live vicariously through the music, the clothes, the jewelry, and the lifestyle.

The strength of the myth is evidenced by its acceptance around the world by young, mostly middle-class consumers who want to show their disdain for authority and assert their independence from the mainstream society. That it came to the world from the United States is no coincidence. The world has always been captivated by American cultural products, and the gangsta rap myth coincided perfectly with the global growth and power of the U.S. media, both traditional TV, particularly cable channels like CNN, and new technologies such as the Internet.

The Birth of Gangsta Rap

If every good story needs a villain, then the one in *Hip-Hop, Inc.* is Suge Knight, who turned Death Row Records into a music company that would make Tony Soprano proud. In many ways,

Knight came to personify gangsta rap, and when he departed the scene, much of the muscle went out of the genre. But although he may have been the living embodiment of gangsta music, he didn't start it.

In 1989 Miami's Luther Campbell paved the way for gangsta rap's excesses with an obscenity-laced, almost pornographic album from a group called 2 Live Crew. He got tons of press and made millions of dollars until the lawsuits poured in and the barred appearances increased. In 1995 Campbell had to file for bankruptcy.

As the 1980s came to a close, a South Central Los Angeles group called N.W.A. (Niggaz With Attitude) changed everything.

Dr. Dre: Straight Outta' Compton—and Into the Suburbs

Ruthless Records, the label that really got gangsta rap off the ground, got an unlikely start. Barely known producer and performer Dr. Dre was in jail for a string of unpaid tickets on his car and needed someone with nine hundred dollars to bail him out. When the first person he called turned him down, the second one, Eric "Eazy-E" Wright agreed—on one condition: Dre would have to work off his debt by producing tracks for the new record label Wright was forming. Dre agreed and the arrangement eventually led to the recording of N.W.A.'s *Straight Outta Compton.* It was the work of a loose-knit group of five teenagers, including reluctant rapper Eazy-E himself. Critics alternately called it "a work of revolutionary genius" and "reprehensible trash with no redeeming value."

The album was shocking in its level of profanity and violence. Despite no radio airplay and a ban on MTV, the album sold three million copies and stirred up a storm of protest, especially for the song "Fuck tha Police." Law enforcement groups protested, parents protested, and the FBI even sent the label a letter expressing its displeasure about the song. All this publicity naturally made the album a "must-have" item for rebellious teens. Soon N.W.A.'s cartoonish violence could be heard booming out of car stereos in even the whitest gated communities of Middle America. Gangsta rap had hit the mainstream.

N.W.A. woke the music industry to the huge commercial possibilities of hard-core rap. Jerry Heller, who bankrolled Ruthless Records along with Eazy-E, told the *Los Angeles Times,* "The economics of it were staggering. Just staggering. If you were with Warner Brothers, for example, and you sold 500,000 records, they might drop you from the label. The way we were doing it, if you sold 200,000 records you made a quarter million dollars. And you made it right there. We'd take the check to the bank, cash it and split it up on the corner."

Ice Cube left N.W.A. and Ruthless in 1989, after being frustrated with the way those checks were being split. He began a highly successful solo career and has since created a movie and music corporation of his own. Dre split from Ruthless in 1992 to join up with a burly bodyguard named Suge Knight.

Marion "Suge" Knight Muscles In

In the book *Have Gun Will Travel: The Spectacular Rise and Violent Fall of Death Row Records,* author Ronin Ro describes Suge Knight as "an imposing former bodyguard who stood 6 foot three inches tall, weighed over 320 pounds, and stared at people as if measuring them for a coffin."

Rappers seem to have a universal fascination for *The Godfather* movies and *Scarface.* Knight's rapid rise to power and riches shows what one can accomplish in the short term by using the methods of those Mafia figures: intimidation, brutality, physical threats, and "enforcers" on the payroll. In its first four years of operation, his Death Row label sold more than eighteen million albums and grossed around $325 million. It established the careers of Dr. Dre, Snoop Dog, Tha Dogg Pound, and Tupac Shakur and became the most lucrative rap label in history.

In the long term, however, running a label like a gang operation is not a sustainable way to run an enterprise that operates in the public eye. Former artist Snoop Dogg eventually left Death Row and signed up with Master P's No Limit label. He later told VH-1, "From Master P I learned what to do. From Suge I learned what *not* to do. Suge Knight was a crook."

Death Row Records was founded on violence, and that set the stage for how the company would operate throughout its history. Knight reportedly obtained the contracts for his first three acts, Dr. Dre, The D.O.C., and Miche'lle, after threatening their current contract owner, Eazy-E of Ruthless Records, with baseball bats and pipes. During that fateful meeting, while backed up by a whole crew of gang members, Knight told Eazy-E, "We know where your mother lives." The papers were signed. Just like that, the artists signed to Ruthless Records were now signed to Death Row.

Eazy-E later filed suit over the contracts and ended up with a royalty agreement from Interscope on anything that Dre produced. The other partner in Ruthless, Jerry Heller, began stashing guns all over his home and office and hired two dozen guards after being continually threatened by Knight and his crew. One of Heller's assistants quit, saying in his resignation letter that he feared for the lives of his wife and child.

The Beginning

Little did his parents know where his life was headed when they nicknamed young Marion Jr. "Sugar Bear," for his gentle disposition. Marion "Suge" Knight grew up in Compton, the blighted, gang-running area of Los Angeles that was the stage set for N.W.A.'s groundbreaking gangsta rap albums and the real set of the 1992 riots touched off by the Rodney King trial.

Knight dreamed of bigger and better things from the beginning. He often told his mother, "One day I'm going to live in a house with a second floor and lots of cars." He played football in high school and got a scholarship to UNLV in Las Vegas. In his senior year he was drafted by the Los Angeles Rams and never finished college. The football career was short-lived, however, and he was soon cut from the team. His temper and violent nature started to reveal themselves soon after. His girlfriend got a restraining order after he vandalized her car and threatened her if she left him. He was arrested in Las Vegas on a variety of assault charges after shattering a man's jaw and pistol-whipping him, but was let go with a fine and three years' probation.

He returned to Los Angeles and worked as a bodyguard. Through his connections, he hatched a plan to get to Dr. Dre and convince him to break away from his current label. He felt that most hard-core rappers were really "too soft" and that someone like him, who was willing to back up threats with action during negotiations, could become a major force in the industry. As nutty as it sounded, Knight's drive and ambition made it happen and Death Row was born.

Success by Intimidation

Fittingly, the financing deal that really got Death Row going was signed in a jail, where Knight was spending one of his first incarcerations. A known drug dealer named Michael Harris put up $1.5 million in financing in return for sharing in management and profits. Harris reportedly never even got his initial investment back, but after repeated threats of violence, he dropped his claims.

After being turned down by the major record labels, partly because of the way Knight obtained his artist contracts, he and partner Dr. Dre got a bite at Interscope. The label put up $10 million in financing after hearing the recordings of Dr. Dre's solo debut, *The Chronic*. The album was a huge success. Not only was it a top-ten album for eight straight months, but it also sold three million copies and is still a strong catalog item today. It is continually hailed as a classic and usually makes any list of the best hip-hop albums in history.

Knight was a quick learner, and it didn't take him long to figure out how the music business game was played. As former Snoop Doggy Dog bodyguard McKinley "Malik" Lee said, "He was a clever student, soaking up each and every experience or encounter and then throwing out the stuff he didn't need."

Knight tried to have a hand in everything: songwriting, production, promotion, and videos. From the beginning, he wanted his organization to be seen as the Motown of the 1990s, a black-owned enterprise cranking out hits recorded by black artists and producers. He signed the artists to deals that also made him their manager, creating an obvious conflict of interest. He also made himself "executive producer" of each album and held on to the publishing, giving himself a cut of the action from every performance and radio airing. When he signed rapper CPO (aka Boss Hog), payment was six thousand dollars up front and one thousand per month. But since CPO was on a form of welfare at the time, he jumped on the deal, signing over all of his publishing and giving up all rights for his contribution to a movie soundtrack. Like so many performers who took on lousy deals because they were broke, CPO replied, "A thousand dollars a month for me was great!"

The Thug Life Meets the Office

Instead of the record label offering a way out of the ghetto, Knight seemed intent on bring the ghetto's gang violence into the business. He hired a cocaine dealer on probation, with no music business experience, to serve as president. At a platinum album party for Dr. Dre, on Dre's birthday, Knight made the rounds with a platter and hit up guests for a "donation" to fund the party. He seemed to model his life after the gangster movie stars he admired, even buying the Las Vegas house Martin Scorsese used as Frank "Lefty" Rosenthal's home in the movie *Casino*. He also bought a nightclub from a known East Coast Mafia family.

The Death Row office was manned by ex-convict Bloods

(members of one of LA's two rival gangs) at all times, and Knight painted his office red—the gang color of the Bloods. One staff member said the office had the feel of a prison cellblock, with employees and office visitors being shaken down for lunch money. Anyone who disagreed with Knight or crossed him in some way was liable to end up with a broken nose, broken ribs, or worse. While staffers were filing papers and trying to make phone calls, someone Knight had a beef with would be yelling for help from a locked storage room.

The tales of violence were so frequent that it mattered little which incidents were exaggerated and which were just routine business. Knight supposedly held Vanilla Ice in the air outside a hotel balcony to get him to sign over publishing on his songs. When artist Warren G left Death Row and then disparaged Knight in the press, Knight sent a squad of his goons to beat up the artist at his home. When he felt like the head of the rap promotion department at parent label Interscope wasn't giving his artists the proper respect, Knight pulled the executive out of a meeting, choked him against the wall, and had his bodyguards beat him up.

After Knight took over management for Jodeci and Mary J. Blige, he got their royalty rate raised by meeting with their label head in a men's room, having the Death Row goons hold the executive's head over a toilet bowl and threatening him with a beating. In yet another incident, when a reporter for the *New Yorker* was interviewing Knight in his office and asked the wrong question, his face got held over a tank full of piranhas. After one rap artist manager got the better of Knight in a fight at a club, both he and his girlfriend were mysteriously murdered a few weeks later.

When Knight wasn't attracting violence, he stirred it up himself. He was frequently blamed for setting up the East Coast/West Coast rap rivalry with Puff Daddy's Bad Boy label and publicly criticized them whenever he got the chance. At a 1995 party he and his henchmen shook down an independent record promoter to get the home addresses of Puff Daddy and his mother. When the promoter wouldn't comply, he was beat up before being rescued by arriving police. The promoter eventually received a six-hundred-thousand-dollar settlement after filing suit and leaving immediately for Jamaica. When one of Death Row's artists included some East Coast rappers on his album, Knight confronted him in a meeting and had his crew deliver a beating. The artist's album was never released.

While he denies it vehemently, Knight has frequently been implicated in the murders of both Death Row artist Tupac Shakur (who had grumbled about wanting to leave the label) and his East Coast rival The Notorious B.I.G. (to make it all look like an East Coast/West Coast rivalry killing).

Death Row Hits the Jackpot

Despite all the trouble he created, Suge Knight was not stingy with his money. He did pump a lot into the community and into charity—much of it quietly. He hosted meals for single mothers on Mother's Day and set up a fund to care for soul singers left poor after their careers were finished. He sponsored a huge turkey dinner for the needy in South Central Los Angeles on Thanksgiving each year.

In the beginning, Death Row plowed most of the early royalties from a movie soundtrack and Dr. Dre's debut back into the label. As more artists released albums and sales took off, the finances of Death Row improved dramatically.

During the recording of Snoop Doggy Dog's debut album, the crew was ejected from nine different studios because of all the partying, drug use, and gang presence. Eventually the album was completed, however, and became a smash hit, selling more than 4.5 million copies. Knight had his next big star and big money started turning into huge money. When the royalties started pouring in, Knight took a page from the Motown playbook and gave his artists fancy cars to distract them from the lack of cash they were making from their recordings. Death Row artists were suddenly driving around the 'hood in a Lexus or a decked-out SUV.

More hits piled up, mostly violent gangsta rap, and Death Row became known as the baddest record label around. Knight reportedly was not interested in Tupac Shakur at first. But when Shakur began to get arrested and get into brawls, Knight decided he was perfect for Death Row's image. A deal was inked while Shakur was in prison. When he got out, his 1996 Death Row album, *All Eyez on Me*, sold five million copies in its first few months of release.

Death Row signed several non-rap artists, but only one of them was white. She was the daughter of LA district attorney Mark Longo, who had earlier prosecuted Knight's case. Knight then reached out to Longo for help in renting a beach house and ended up with Longo's Malibu beach house. The obvious conflict of interest paid off for a while, until Longo's superiors found out about the arrangements and the press got wind of it. Longo was reassigned.

The Beginning of the End

In 1996 the original partners in the label, Knight and Dr. Dre, parted ways. Dre had been drifting away from the label for some time, unhappy with all the negativity and violence that was ever present in the office, at award shows, and on tours. He announced that he was leaving Death Row to start his own company, with a deal through Interscope.

On the sales side, everything looked rosy. The top three rap albums of 1996 were all from Death Row: two from Tupac Shakur and the sophomore release from Snoop Dogg. Despite all the money coming in, however, Death Row's finances were a mess. The label easily spent as much as it made living the high life all around, and its account was continually overdrawn. It didn't help that Knight had entrusted the label's books as well as his own to a flashy accountant who had never passed his CPA exam. The accountant lived like he was part of the team, spending as freely as Knight, and reportedly embezzled more than $4 million. At one point Death Row had outstanding American Express charges of $1,574,992.

The bottom fell out in October 1996. While on parole, Knight was accused of beating someone up in a Las Vegas hotel lobby—an action caught on the hotel's surveillance video. Tupac Shakur also participated in the beating, one of his last actions before being killed in a drive-by shooting that same night, with Knight in the driver's seat. For violating parole, after already missing several scheduled drug tests, Knight was sentenced to nine years in prison and spent the rest of the 1990s locked up. As soon as he was sent away to jail, Death Row began to crumble. As Snoop Dog's bodyguard Malik Lee said in his book, *Chosen by Fate: My Life inside Death Row Records,* "I knew he would end up filthy rich or locked behind bars. Both premonitions came true."

First, the FBI stepped up its investigation of the label's business practices. The DEA and IRS soon jumped in. The label was late on its rent for its offices. It was five albums behind on its obligations to Interscope, for albums where the advances had already been cashed. American Express sued to recover the more than $1.5 million it was still owed.

Tupac Shakur's mother, Arfeni Shakur, went on a lawsuit rampage soon after her son was killed, suing both Death Row and Interscope for back music royalties and merchandising royalties. With Interscope stepping in and heat coming from Arfeni's appearances on national TV, she received more than $5 million and the promise of a higher royalty rate on future sales. On top of all this, producers and rappers who hadn't gotten paid what they were promised started to sue.

In 1997 several groups turned up the heat on the corporate owners and distributors of Interscope: MCA/Universal, recently purchased by liquor company Seagram. In order to distance itself from the gangsta rap controversy and appease shareholders, Seagram severed its ties with Interscope. Interscope then abandoned Death Row. The label was now on death row itself.

Don't Call It a Comeback

In 2001 Knight was released from prison after nearly five years and tried to restart his business by signing several new artists. In December of that year, however, he was jailed again for violating his probation. After release from that stint, he was arrested and jailed yet again in 2003.

Knight was released on April 23, 2004. It didn't last, however. Less than a year later, he was arrested after police pulled him over for making an unsafe U-turn and found marijuana in his vehicle. After a few days in jail, he was fitted with an electronic monitoring device and placed under house arrest.

In 2005 he could walk free and travel. But in August, the same month he appeared on the cover of *The Source* magazine and talked about another comeback, he was shot in the leg at a party in Miami.

Unlike the other moguls profiled in this book, Suge Knight never tried to extend his empire much beyond the music business. He owned a car customization shop called Let It Ride, but that was about it for outside ventures. As a result, when Death Row began to implode while he was in jail, he had little to fall back on when he got out. He now has more notoriety than power.

In the book *Chosen by Fate*, cowriter Frank B. Williams said of the Death Row story, "At its apex, it's an amazing example of the bootstrap philosophy, driven by a healthy ambition we can all appreciate. But in the shadows of the company's great legacy, in the dark dregs there was violence, dissension, and murder."

"Rip out this page in the history books and put it somewhere safe," he says. "Make it a reminder of life's great possibilities and its worst dangers."

Gangsta Rap Today

As Death Row started to die, other labels took over. Two brand new moguls, Master P and Damon Dash, quickly filled the void.

Dr. Dre proved he had better sense and more staying power than anyone. He launched the careers of Eminem and 50 Cent and is still one of the hottest producers in the business. (See chapter 11, "Hip-Hop Nation: 'What Else?'")

These days, the genre of gangsta rap has outlived Ruthless Records, Master P's original No Limit Records, and Death Row. Violent rap albums have managed to endure periodic flare-ups of protest and are now routinely released by divisions of some of the world's biggest companies, like Sony, Time-Warner, and Bertelsmann. Viacom-owned MTV and VH-1 continue to play the glorified-violence videos, and gangsta rapper 50 Cent is the best-selling artist of the mid-2000s, period.

● The Rap Backlash: Who Can Change the Channel?

Is rap still "the black CNN" that Chuck D of Public Enemy once claimed it to be?

As Ta-Nehisi Coates noted in the *Village Voice*, gangsta rap lyrics about shootouts in the street are now more fantasy than reality. "The streets that gangsta rappers claim as their source are no longer as angry as they are sad. A true narrative of 'the streets' and the black men who inhabit them," she continues, "would depict a deadbeat ex-con, fleeing mounting child support, unable to find work, and disconnected from the lives of his kids. It would chronicle his gradual slide off the American radar even as his mother, daughter, and girlfriend (not wife) make inroads. It's a story that doesn't lend itself to romance."

Other black social critics are noting the negative effect the music has in keeping black society at the bottom economically. M. K. Asante Jr., writing in *USA Today*, argued that, "The truth, for many African-Americans younger than 30 who invariably belong to the 'Hip-Hop Generation,' is that the rap music of today is inglorious. It's not merely because the lyrics are no longer about knowledge and pride disguised in urban pentameter, but also because today's rap betrays the very people who are part of the hip-hop culture. Young blacks, for example, are unjustly profiled as a result of rap's stigma."

According to Jimmy Iovine, the head of Interscope—once Suge Knight's major label partner—the record labels were and are simply responding to demand. As Iovine told PBS's *Frontline*, "We put out thousands of records by thousands of different types of musicians. And hip-hop was music of the kids. They demanded it, believe me. The industry did not want it to happen. The industry did not state, 'Let's get into the hip-hop business or the rap business.' That was absolutely not the case. The kids drove that movement."

Much of the gangsta rap persona has involved picking fights and having someone to publicly criticize. Death Row's artists usually had their sights set on the East Coast, on a mega-successful enterprise run by a man named Puff Daddy.

Some critics say that hip-hop is an attack on decades of black progress, noting that hardened criminals are celebrated as "keeping it real," while successful black lawyers or doctors are ribbed as being "too white." In the *Memphis Commercial Appeal*, music promoter John M. Shaw pinned the blame on market forces. "Negativity sells, and there is no shortage of buyers."

Rap's critics grow old and gray waiting for big corporations such as Warner Music or Sony/BMG to change the lyrics. As Jeff Clanagan of Code Black Media says about how blacks are portrayed in the media, "We don't control the networks and the content that goes out—the conglomerates do."

But Asante puts the blame on the music itself, saying rap music has gotten stuck in a creative rut, mindlessly cranking out the same material that worked ten years ago. "Rap music tends to blare out redundant, glossy messages of violence without consequence, misogyny and conspicuous consumption. As a result, rap's once-defiant message has slowly deteriorated."

Until the black moguls take control of the situation themselves—as Kanye West looks to be doing with G.O.O.D. Music—the lyrics will be stuck in a cycle of retrograde gang-banging, pistol-shooting, and crime boasting. Whoever steps up and changes the channel will likely find a lucrative market anomaly to exploit.

PUFF DADDY, SEAN JOHN, P. DIDDY, DIDDY

The Man Is the Brand

My flow, my show brought me the doe
That bought me all my fancy things
My crib, my cars, my pools, my jewels

—50 CENT
"In Da Club," from the album
Get Rich or Die Tryin'

A Walking Brand

Diddy. The obvious comparison is Madonna. A star known by only one name. Madonna, master of reinvention. She seems to change her persona (or brand) as often as her clothes. She is the highest earning female singer/entertainer of the past twenty-some years, worth at least $200 million. She is also the personification of paradox: a work-for-hire singer who owns her own production management companies; an exceptional actress with neither extraordinary talent or beauty; a pin-up sex symbol who authors children's books. Madonna has had the longest-lasting versatile career based on multiple identity changes: from glam rock to Monroe retro, from sex goddess to spiritual advisor to the masses.

But while Madonna keeps her name and constantly changes her image, Diddy has done the reverse—keeping his bad-boy image and constantly changing his name. Diddy's name changes, like

Madonna's image changes, defy all business logic. How does he get away with it?

A better comparison for Diddy is Ol' Blue Eyes, Frank Sinatra, says Bruce Hinton, a now retired executive from the Universal Music Group with direct ties to Sinatra. Hinton worked in record promotion with Reprise in Los Angeles in the 1960s, and was present during the recording sessions for "Strangers in the Night," Sinatra's surprise number one hit. Hinton saw firsthand the mastery of Sinatra, both in the studio and in the marketplace. He recognizes many of the same traits in Diddy.

"When P Diddy leaves his house, he is a walking brand," says Hinton. Like Sinatra, he says, "Sean is highly stylized, highly individualistic. Being decked out, dressed the way he is, he's not like any other celebrity." Like Sinatra, says Hinton, "Sean Combs has his own identity. I think that's extremely clever." And, like Sinatra, Hinton says, Combs knows his market well.

"The whole rap arena has embraced the white suburban market now. Every kid wants their own kind of music, not their parents music. Rap came along at a perfect time. A whole new audience out there today is happy to have music that their parents don't understand or appreciate." Just like Ol' Blue Eyes.

Sean Combs, Puff Daddy, P. Diddy, and now just Diddy: they have all come to mean "unique." As Hinton says, in most photos Diddy is looking stylish and decked-out, but one particular photo is the most telling. He wears a sleeveless T-shirt that reads, I AM THE AMERICAN DREAM. Diamond bracelets, a platinum necklace, and a watch that costs more than most people's cars are the punctuation. Like Sinatra, Diddy has become a walking brand.

Hinton isn't the only one to draw the comparison to Sinatra. Diddy uses it himself. As Diddy told *Forbes* magazine in one of his first major interviews in the established business press: "I'm the black Sinatra." (See "The Black Sinatra" on the following page.) By 1997 Combs had already joined the "rat pack" of the hip-hop moguls.

The Black Sinatra

When Rob LaFranco first interviewed Sean Combs in 1998 for *Forbes*, the hip-hop mogul said something that has stayed with LaFranco ever since: "I'm the black Sinatra."

During his eight-year stint in the 1990s as *Forbes* magazine's lead writer on media coverage, including the movies, the Internet, and music, LaFranco became one of the first mainstream business reporters to buck what was then conventional wisdom in the financial press. Instead, he wrote in-depth, pioneering features about the giant potential of the hip-hop moguls, including but not limited to Sean Combs and Russell Simmons.

And Diddy was not the only admirer of everything Sinatra: tough, connected, ostentatious with his wealth. While Sinatra went out of fashion years ago, the street-tough moguls have always admired Frank's reputed Mob ties, as well as his unique ability to rule several areas of show business with an iron hand, and the hip-hop attraction to the Sinatra legacy is clear.

"They're brazen about it," LaFranco says of the moguls' purely capitalistic aim of amassing wealth. "I don't know why, but their focus is materialism. Bling is out of control, it's over the top now." All of these factors add to the mystique of the moguls, as well as to their cachet in Hollywood. But LaFranco goes further, asking, "Why did Puffy become so famous? It's because he embodies every hope and dream of ghetto kids."

LaFranco faced resistance within the editorial offices of *Forbes*, where he says his bosses at first disagreed with his vision of the future business and financial impacts of men who were the progenitors of an entirely new musical genre and whose acts had odd names such as Biggie Smalls, Mystikal, or Xscape, stage sobriquets that, as *The Wall Street Journal* scoffed, "look like typos."

"At the time, everyone at the magazine was saying to go negative [on the moguls]," LaFranco says. But he refused. He knew he was onto something; much of his vision came from an abiding love for an entirely new music that was strong on social commentary and tailor-made for an increasingly global music marketplace. He looked beyond the hip-hop hype and saw the emergence of savvy Wall Street instincts as the moguls developed their empires.

Since Combs and LaFranco first spoke in 1998, Diddy has seen music become less and less a part of his bottom line. "What he's done since then has astounded me," LaFranco says. Diddy built on his production talents to enter a new arena and make even more money. Most mainstream producers of pop and R&B are fairly anonymous, behind-the-scenes folks. Not so in the highly collaborative world of hip-hop recording, where the role of the producer may well be every bit as important—perhaps more important—than that of the artist.

"Where Puffy is making his money now is in producing. He's getting as much as $150,000 per track," LaFranco says. His production clients have included Mary J. Blige, Boyz II Men, Mariah Carey, Faith Evans, Jay-Z, and MC Lyte, Notorious B.I.G., and Usher. LaFranco points out that a track is a song on an album; albums will typically have between ten and fifteen tracks, so that if Combs produced all twelve tracks on an album, he would pocket a cool $1.8 million for his efforts.

Madonna is probably jealous. Sinatra would be proud.

1997: The Arrival of Puff Daddy

"Puff Daddy" Combs ruled the charts and the media in 1997. Between his own album and the songs from others on his Bad Boy label, he touched one-third of the top one hundred singles that year. Nearly a decade later, Sean Combs—once Puff Daddy and now Diddy—is still "ghetto fabulous." These days he doesn't just grace the pages of entertainment magazines. He is just as likely to show up in *Inc., Fortune, Forbes,* or *Time,* being celebrated for his business success, not his music.

Diddy Joins the Hip-Hop Serial Entrepreneurs

One of America's foremost experts on entrepreneurship is John Nesheim, consultant, Cornell University business school professor, and author of *High Tech Start Up: The Complete Handbook for Creating Successful New High Tech Companies.* Nesheim says that Simmons, Dash, Miller, and Diddy all exhibit the characteristics of the classic *serial entrepreneur.* "A serial entrepreneur," he says, "is someone who is constantly creating new businesses, often one right after another. Some entrepreneurs have one idea, start one company and then call it quits. Serial entrepreneurs, on the other hand, almost can't stop creating exciting new enterprises.

"The other characteristic of true serial entrepreneurs," says Nesheim, "is they don't get their egos wrapped up in the business. They make extensive use of their social and business networks to push the limits of the new enterprise, but if it doesn't work, they move on quickly. Some one-time entrepreneurs will let a failure get in their way emotionally. They can't reconcile a business failure. They take it personally and can't separate the business from themselves personally. So when they fail at something, it's usually the end. Not the serial entrepreneur. They just start all over again. They never seem to wear out."

The process of empire building, adding another responsibility to an already hectic schedule, or even the occasional failure, never seems to wear out Sean Combs. There are always more projects in the works. He owns two *Justin's* restaurants, in New York and Atlanta, named after his son. He also runs Blue Flame, the marketing branch of Bad Boy Entertainment, which has teamed up with two major ad agencies. He was invited to give a keynote speech at the Cellular Telecommunications and Internet Association convention, speaking about the fusion of handsets and hip-hop culture. Naturally, he will be releasing his own line of fashionable cell phones.

He has a television production deal with MTV, a movie production deal with Paramount, and an ongoing string of music production jobs. An acclaimed acting career has put him in an Oscar Award–winning movie and a Tony Award–winning Broadway play. As a musical artist and producer, he has won a shelf full of awards and a wall of platinum albums. His clothing company is closing in on a half billion dollars in revenue. Somehow, he also found time to train for and finish the New York Marathon in 2003 and host the MTV Video Music Awards in 2005.

The Early Entrepreneur

Sean Combs was born in Harlem and lived there until he was thirteen, but spent his teen years in the New York suburb of Mount Vernon. His father was killed when he was three and his sister was a newborn, leaving his mother to work hard to make ends meet. Little Sean started earning his own money as soon as he was able. He was only eleven when he got his first job on a paper route, after begging the boss for a chance to show what he could do.

While growing up, he was able to see live rap shows from Run-D.M.C., LL Cool J, and KRS-One. He became enamored with the whole culture and the business behind the performances. He attended a private boys' school, Mt. Saint Michael's Academy. When angry, he would huff and puff with exasperation. He also puffed out his chest on the football field to give more heft to his small frame, leading to the "puffy" nickname.

Combs practiced his dance moves constantly and became known by his friends as a good dancer. He eventually auditioned for some music videos and ended up performing as an extra in videos by Doug E. Fresh, Babyface, and the Fine Young Cannibals.

The College Hustler

After graduating from high school, Combs attended Howard University in Washington, DC. While there he kept tabs on the music business in New York. He saw the power and charisma exuded by music executives, including his eventual mentor, Andre Harrell, and decided he wanted to be a part of that.

Meanwhile, his ability to spot an opportunity and make a buck was showing up on campus. He was known to peddle term papers, sodas, and T-shirts—whatever jumped out at him as a profitable niche to exploit. When some rebellious students took over an administrative building, Combs put magazine and newspaper clips about the event into a poster-sized collage and sold copies to the sit-in participants.

Soon Combs began staging DC parties with a very New York City flavor. To distinguish his first event and start things off with a bang, he talked several rap stars into attending, including Heavy D, Slick Rick, and Doug E. Fresh. At one point he was promoting a party every week and was pulling in big crowds. His studies started to suffer, but at the same time he was starting to see that a four-year degree program was going to prolong the period before he could start reaching his goals.

As he said in a VH-1 interview, "I had always admired people that were doing the behind-the-scenes stuff, but also I admired the producers. I admired Quincy Jones and Berry Gordy. And I admired Russell Simmons and Run-D.M.C., Michael Jackson and Dr. Dre. And one thing that all these people had in common was, they knew how to package a lifestyle and a point of view and package black American culture in a way where it organically was good business . . . Everybody passed the baton and I was blessed to one day get the baton passed to me."

After several failed attempts to get a job in New York in the music business, he changed tactics. He decided to get his foot in the door with an internship. After being turned down at Def Jam after an interview, he leaned on acquaintance Heavy D to get him an interview at Uptown Records. Heavy D arranged a meeting with Andre Harrell of Uptown (a subsidiary of MCA), and at nineteen years old, Sean Combs started working at Uptown as an intern two days a week, commuting back and forth from

DC. He dressed well, worked very hard, and took copious notes on how everything worked. Most of his days were spent doing the usual grunt work, but he impressed Harrell as "the hardest-working intern ever."

Seizing the Moment

Combs eventually dropped out of Howard, started working at Uptown full time, and moved into Andre Harrell's home in New Jersey. Ironically, Andre had gotten a similar start, living in Russell Simmons's New Jersey home in 1984 while working for Def Jam. Suddenly Combs had a real job and a room in a nice house with a pool. He also now had the chance to expand his network and meet many movers and shakers in the music industry.

Under Harrell's grooming, Combs was handling a lot of artist and repertoire (A&R) duties for Uptown acts, working with artists such as Mary J. Blige, Heavy D, and Father MC, occasionally getting production credit. When the head of A&R resigned in 1991, Combs got the vacant position. He combined a good ear with plenty of marketing savvy. The first project he really took on as his own, Jodeci, became an unqualified success. In a sign of things to come, he spent as much time on their look as their music, and remixed existing tracks to create even bigger hits. He also sent squads of teens to nightclubs and told them to pack the floor when a Jodeci track was played. Jodeci took time to get started, but eventually all the groundwork paid off. Their debut album hit the top twenty and went double platinum. Combs was suddenly a producer with a "hot hand" as well as a label executive. The added producer title was significant, as it meant that he would earn a portion of the royalties on all sales. This would form a major part of his financial empire in the coming years.

One of Combs's signature tactics became pairing an artist with an established name. He would put a "guest appearance" from a new act on a track from a successful artist, thereby providing an introduction to consumers. Once the new act's own single or album hit, there was already some built-in awareness. He had success with this at Uptown, and it became a huge factor in a long list of successful acts at his own label later, time and time again.

Relentless Preparation

On the surface, few would argue that fellow New Yorkers Rudolph Giuliani and P. Diddy have much in common. But they do. Their fundamental beliefs about leadership, management, and success have uncanny parallels. One of the most striking similarities between the philosophies of the two men is what Giuliani calls "relentless preparation." If you want to succeed, argues the former mayor of New York, now a wildly successful global entrepreneur, you have to know more about the subject than anyone else. "You prepare for the unexpected," he says, "by preparing for everything else."

Combs is clearly prepared for the unexpected. His compulsive, relentless nature was evident from the start. He always has multiple projects in the works. While he was working at Uptown, he started arranging nightclub events each week called "Daddy's House." Appointed a vice president at the label at just twenty-three, he started wearing a diamond-studded medallion in the shape of a man's head. He said it represented Lazarus, a man who had been reborn. From a marketing standpoint, he was earning a reputation as a winner. He believed that success came from giving people what they wanted, not from anything revolutionary. He simply paid attention to what people were listening to and tried to distill it all into one package. More than anyone else at the time, he found a way to combine street style and culture, club energy, middle-class values, and a feeling of upward mobility.

In his view, Mary J. Blige embodied it all. His boss, Andre Harrell, had coined the phrase "ghetto fabulous" earlier, and Combs felt that Blige fit the term exactly. Her 1992 debut album sold more than two million copies and reached number six on the pop album chart.

The Birth of Bad Boy

The key to the executive promotion in Puff Daddy's eyes, however, was assurance that his own Bad Boy Entertainment company would be launched by Uptown. Bad Boy would be Combs's own management, record, and production company. Publicly the move was the result of Combs's success with Jodeci and Mary J. Blige. Privately, many speculated that it was a way to separate Combs's free-spending ways from Harrell's own books, as Harrell was tired of running into trouble with parent company MCA.

The arrangement didn't last long, however, and in July 1993, Harrell decided that Uptown wasn't big enough for the both of them. Puff Daddy was fired. Whether the apprentice had grown bigger than the master or Harrell was just tired of the attitude and the money battles, it was clear to everyone that the clashes were growing more frequent, including battles over musical direction. The sounds Combs was pursuing with his new rap from signing Biggie Smalls didn't fit with what Uptown was doing.

At first Combs ran Bad Boy out of his mother's Westchester home, with a handful of employees. It didn't take long for him to work out another deal, however. Bad Boy signed up with Arista and legendary music executive Clive Davis. It was simply a matter of asking Sean the right questions. While other labels had asked Combs a lot of questions about money, Clive Davis asked him what kind of music he wanted to make. Davis struck Combs as a man who knew where the priorities should be, and the deal was done: $15 million for distribution rights, with Combs's mother, Janice, posted as the official owner of Bad Boy Entertainment. Sean Combs started out with an annual salary of seven hundred thousand dollars per year.

Hands-On Hit Machine

With the chance to shape Biggie Smalls, better known as the Notorious B.I.G., Combs took "hands-on management" to a new level, supervising every aspect of every song to make sure it was as good, and as commercial, as it could possibly be. From the beginning, Combs has micromanaged everything. He wants a hand in every aspect of every project he's involved with: picking the office furniture, designing the stationery, shaping the drumbeat on a single, choosing what the artist should wear in the video. Every scenario is considered and debated. As Combs told VH-1:

> I'm definitely the biggest fan of Berry Gordy and his artist development and his attention to detail. I think that if Berry had to sew one of the Supremes' outfits he would have, and that's the same thing I would do. If I have to jump in my car and go shopping to style a video, to this day, I will do things like that. If I have to button your shirt or tie your tie, I will do that. And I try to help the artists understand it's not just about what you create. You have to bring something out of an artist and have them understand it so they can live it and be it when it's time for them to be an artist.

This control extended to his other artists as well: Craig Mack, Faith Evans, Total, and 112. For everyone on his label, Combs was the executive producer, stylist, publicist, and strategist rolled into one.

Despite a grueling workload that would have quickly worn down most anyone, Combs managed to keep adding outside production projects. He was getting calls from the top-tier artists and managers and ended up producing tracks for Lil' Kim, TLC, Mariah Carey, Boyz II Men, SWV, and Aretha Franklin.

Over the years, Combs's production style has been criticized by many for being watered-down and predictable, often relying on samples from familiar hits of the past. But there's no denying that it worked from a commercial standpoint. Many of the tracks he produced quickly vaulted to the top of the charts and could be heard blasting out of car radios, boom boxes, and nightclub speakers across the country, and across the world. Whether by design or as a bonus, these tracks became a sort of Puff Daddy pension. If he was credited as one of the songwriters on a track, he shared royalties from all publishing activity: radio play, samples, cover versions, or licensing in movies or commercials, as well as royalties from sales of the singles and albums. As a producer, he got another cut again. On top of his other income, some of these hits from ten years ago are certainly still generating significant income today.

Regardless of how the process worked, there was no denying that Bad Boy was onto something. From 1994 through 1997 the label reportedly racked up over $100 million in sales, an impressive accomplishment for a start-up label with no catalog sales.

Puff Daddy the Artist

Combs seemed to have a hand in every aspect of his artists' success, but he also showed up on songs as a guest rapper and could be seen dancing in more than a few videos. The natural evolution was an album of his own. If Combs truly did have the magic touch when it came to putting out songs that people wanted to hear, it wouldn't be much of a stretch to do an album of hits on his own, or so his thinking went.

The Puff Daddy debut was a record-breaking smash. The album's biggest single, "I'll Be Missing You" was number one on six different *Billboard* charts for eight consecutive weeks and was number one for eleven weeks on the pop singles chart. It also went to number one in fifteen other countries, from Canada to Greece to New Zealand. The song won a Grammy for Best Rap Performance by a Duo or Group, while *No Way Out* won Best Rap Album. He told VH-1, "Me as an artist is different than me as a businessman. It's like a superstar glow that just takes over your body, and you have to put forth that level of confidence and entertain."

New Decade, New Label Deals

So far this decade, Combs has had more success outside his record label than in it. Arista stopped distributing Bad Boy recordings in 2002 after the head of that label, Clive Davis, was pushed out. Nevertheless, the multiple revenue streams and investments continued to pay off. In 2002 P. Diddy was number twelve on *Fortune* magazine's "America's 40 Richest People Under 40" list.

The departure from Arista was a good one for Combs in the long run, since he walked away with his entire artist roster and rights to 100 percent of his catalog. Combs eventually had to settle for a distribution deal for Bad Boy, and signed a deal for $20 million with Universal in 2003. Since he was unable to sell part of his label, Bad Boy Records was formed as an independent record company. Faith Evans left the label, and 112 tried to, but couldn't get out of their contract.

After shopping around a deal for the Bad Boy label in early 2005, Combs signed a fifty-fifty joint venture deal with Warner Music Group. In making the announcement, Edgar Bronfman Jr., chairman and CEO of Warner Music Group, said of Combs, "His ability to cultivate new artists, combined with his relentless drive, makes Sean one of the entertainment industry's truly gifted and rare talents."

Branching Out in the New Century

Combs has continued to rack up gains as a both a producer and a guest artist on other albums this decade, including work with David Bowie, Britney Spears, and *N Sync. In 2003 he ran in the New York City Marathon and raised more than two million dollars for the educational system for the children of New York. He also donated one million dollars to his alma mater, Howard University, and campaigned hard to increase young voter registrations in the 2004 elections. The ubiquitous T-shirts read "Vote or Die."

At the end of 2004, *Inc.* magazine estimated the Bad Boy empire to be worth $300 million and Combs's personal worth to be even higher. Combs "only" earned an estimated $11.7 million from Bad Boy music in 2004, but he continued to rake in more money from production work, publishing royalties, acting, and now, a successful clothing line.

Diddy the Actor

In a sign that Sean Combs has both boundless energy and an unquenchable restlessness, he has also made his mark as a successful actor. His performance in *Monster's Ball* as the death row inmate Lawrence Musgrove was well received, and the film became an Oscar winner and a commercial success. Paramount Pictures and MTV Films have signed him to develop and star in a heist action-comedy.

He went on to play Walter Lee Younger in the Broadway production of *A Raisin in the Sun,* with Audra McDonald and Phylicia Rashad, both of whom won Tony Awards for their performances. McDonald told *Variety,* "He exceeded my expectations. He has a work ethic unlike any I've ever seen. He is tireless. And he is a cheerleader and a clown." Costar Sanaa Lathan told the *Daily News,* "He's a real mascot. He has an infectious enthusiasm that I've never seen before," while in the *New York Post,* Clive Barnes said, "Let's cut to the chase: Sean Combs is damn good!"

His *Making the Band* series on MTV has had a three-season run. He also signed a "first look" production deal with MTV for further television productions. Of course the bands' albums are all released on Bad Boy.

Combs is a regular on awards shows, often as a host, and he performed during the Super Bowl in 2004. Though he probably didn't need the money, he also starred in a high-profile Diet Pepsi ad campaign that ran during the game.

Keeping Your Eye on the Prize: From Music to Menswear

Heavyweight fighter and now TV pitch man George Foreman won the heavyweight championship of the world twice—twenty years apart! He did it, he says, by sheer determination and "keeping my eye on the prize."

Combs has never lost sight of the prize, either. But at the outset no one guessed that the prize would be more than just entertainment success. And now the obsessive attention to detail, the relentless preparation and hard work has brought him prize-winning success in new endeavors.

Following in the footsteps of Russell Simmons and the Roc-A-Fella partners, Combs has found clothing to be a natural extension of his empire. As always, he thought big from the start. He started looking for an expansion deal soon after starting the line. In 2003 California billionaire Ron Burke invested $100 million in the Sean John clothing business, with the aim of turning the collection into a global, billion-dollar brand.

The Brand's the Man: The Man's Worth Millions

Success has come quickly in this area: the Sean John line had wholesale revenues of $225 million in 2004, with a reported margin of around 10 percent. Combs has become one of America's most bankable brands.

Today most companies are valued by their worth of their brands. In 1960 the market capitalization (the total stock value) of the all the companies on the New York Stock Exchange (NYSE) was roughly equivalent to the value of their physical assets (factories, trucks, etc.). Today the aggregate value of the stocks on the NYSE is three to four times the value of the company's physical assets. What's the difference? The value of their "intellectual property"—in most cases it's their brands.

Brands used to be built with large advertising budgets on TV, newspapers, and magazines. That's how older brands achieved their success. Today, however, the fast-growing brands are those that use new, cross-promotional techniques, like those pioneered by the hip-hop entrepreneurs. *Business Week*, in its annual brand rankings, makes the point succinctly:

> The brands that rose to the top of our ranking [Samsung, eBay, Starbucks] all had widely varied marketing arsenals and were able to unleash different campaigns for different consumers in varied media almost simultaneously. They wove messages over multiple media channels and blurred the lines between ads and entertainment. As a result, these brands can be found in a host of new venues: the Web, live events, cell phones, and handheld computers. Established brands [Coke or Marlboro] achieved their global heft decades ago by the 30-second TV commercial . . . But it's a different world now . . . it's not surprising that there's a new generation of brands . . . [that] have amassed huge global value with little traditional advertising.

Combs has become a master at the new branding, relying not on media advertising, but on cross-promotion and public relations buzz. The fashion line gained a huge boost of cachet in June 2004 when Combs was named "Best Menswear Designer" at the Council of Fashion Designers of America Fashion Awards—the equivalent of an Oscar or Grammy in the fashion world—beating out Ralph Lauren and Michael Kors. He became the first outside celebrity to earn the fashion industry's highest mark of approval, a sign of being embraced as one of its own.

Not content with the early success, Combs launched two new labels, the pricey Sean John Collection, for upscale retailers, and the moderately priced Bad Boy brand for active lifestyles. Sean John also signed licensing deals for tailored clothing, dress shirts, and neckwear, which some analysts predict could put the brand's retail sales over the $500 million mark annually.

Harrell may have coined the phrase "ghetto fabulous," but Combs has lived by it. In his eyes, the idea was to inspire kids in the 'hood to do better, to show them you could achieve success and wealth by legitimate means. "Anyone can do what I have done," he often says. "Kids just need a chance to succeed."

Creating the Category

Critics of hip-hop often argue that "it all sounds the same." Further, they say, the rappers "all look, dress, and act the same." This is bad business, the critics assert, because the individual record labels or performers aren't clearly differentiated. This "sameness" is totally contrary to the strategy that most business people have been taught as marketing dogma for the last thirty years or more.

Conventional business wisdom preaches that there are three interlocking requirements for successful competition against your closest rivals (e.g., 50 Cent vs. LL Cool J). Success, it is said, is achieved by the execution of three things:

- *Differentiate* your product or service at all costs: make sure consumers see your brand and product as clearly different than the competitors' in areas such as price, place of purchase, product design, quality, etc.
- To achieve this differentiation, every product needs a *unique selling proposition* (USP)—the single idea that makes you different.
- Constantly hammer home the USP in advertising. If it works, the business mantra is complete, because you have achieved marketing nirvana, the ultimate goal: *positioning* (getting a unique place in the consumer's mind).

Fortunately for the hip-hop moguls, they weren't handicapped with this thinking. In many product and service "categories," particularly lifestyle and cultural ones, the initial basis of competition is *not* between individual products (Sean John vs. Phat Farm, for example), but *between competing categories* (say, hip-hop vs. rock).

In music, clothes, and related product categories, consumers make lifestyle choices first, then pick the individual brand. As long as the product meets the minimum acceptable attributes of the category (oversized shirts with a music star's name on it), the consumer will buy. Competition between products and brands comes from delivering the most satisfaction, or value, at the best price *within the category*.

Whether the hip-hop entrepreneurs understand this or not (and their strategies, actions, and success indicates they clearly do), from the pioneers such as Russell Simmons to the next wave, such as Diddy, they all *promote the category first and foremost*. Watch any of the moguls, from Diddy to "Fiddy": they sell the category in everything they do. From the beginning with Simmons to today's mogul-wannabes, they talk, look, promote, support, and sell the hip-hop lifestyle.

Stretching the Category

The intuitive understanding of creating a category first and competing on brands second would be enough for books to be written about any group of business entrepreneurs. But the hip-hop moguls took it a step further and continue to do so. Once they had consumers sold on the category, they've worked diligently to *stretch the category* from music to clothes, clothes to jewelry, jewelry to cars, and from cars to credit cards and travel, and beyond.

To be a member of the hip-hop nation, today's consumer must not only listen, look, and drive the lifestyle, they must also do their financing, vacation planning, and whatever else the moguls can convince them belongs in the category. It is a brilliant strategy, with exceptional execution. And they just keep coming.

8

"GHETTO BILL"

Brilliant Vision; Flawless Execution

> "If it don't make dollars, it don't make sense."
>
> —MASTER P

RUSSELL SIMMONS IS revered as the godfather of hip-hop. Sean "Diddy" Combs is unchallenged as its celebrity king. Roc-A-Fella's Damon Dash and Kareem "Biggs" Burke are the crown princes of hip-hop and have captured stories on the pages of hip-hop and business magazines for years. The *New York Times* dubbed Jay-Z "the new boss." Eminem and 50 Cent are the retail aces, holding a commanding lead in the bad boy category. Snoop has taken star billing in TV commercials; and LL Cool J is everywhere: music, movies, TV, and clothing. Missy Elliot and Lil' Kim reign as the queens of hip-hop.

So where does Percy "Master P" Miller fit into all of this? Making trips to the bank, cashing checks, that's where. Very fitting for the man who refers to himself as the "ghetto Bill Gates."

Rulin' the Charts, Rakin' in da Benjamins

In 1999, two years after slick Puff Daddy ruled the charts and made more than $100 million in one year, it was Master P's turn. Miller came out of nowhere and made *Fortune* magazine's list of "America's 40 Richest People Under 40." Popping onto the list at number 29, the rapper was estimated to be worth a staggering $361 million, $57 million of it earned in 1998 alone. *Forbes* named him to their "Top List of Highest Paid Entertainers." For two years, he was recognized by *The Source* magazine as the number one most powerful player in rap music. At one point he even made the *Guinness Book of World Records* as the world's richest entertainer.

What was amazing about this impressive collection of wealth was that he had built up this fortune on his own, while flying under the mainstream radar. Not only was he unknown to most of the readers of *Fortune,* he wasn't even that well known in the entertainment industry outside of rap circles. He wasn't on the cover of gossip magazines or profiled on *Entertainment Tonight.* He put out his stuff, people bought it, and he collected the cash. No big thing.

But suddenly, Master P appeared on the *Fortune* list along with people such as Michael Dell and Jeff Bezos just as the dot-com craze was swinging into full gear. As journalist Marcus Errico said, "The ascension of Master P and his No Limit Enterprises has been as remarkable as any of his computer geek compadres on the various *Fortune* and *Forbes* lists, for his empire was formed with little fanfare."

Bezos, Dell, Miller: Takin' Care of Business

What Master P shares with the likes of Michael Dell and Jeff Bezos, though, goes much deeper than a listing on the world's wealthiest. Both Dell and Bezos had brilliant, world-changing visions of their businesses, and then combined it with something equally special: flawless execution. It's what Elvis always referred to as TCB: takin' care of business.

By all rights, Jeff Bezos, founder of Amazon, was not the one to change the book industry. The industry leaders, Barnes & Noble or Borders should have done that. After all, they held commanding market shares in book selling. But they were too busy looking at the world the way it was instead of dreaming (as President John Kennedy once said) about the way it could be and asking "why not?"

A New York financial analyst with no book industry experience, Bezos looked at his computer screen one day and decided people could order stuff online. But what? He didn't know, but was determined to find out. So he quit his job, went for a drive across the country, and tried to figure out what stuff might sell via the Internet. By the time he reached Redmond, Washington, he had his answer—books. After a rocky start, he changed the book industry by lowering the real costs of books, including the actual sticker price, but more importantly, essentially "reducing the search costs" (the time and effort it takes to find a book).

Selling Books One Detail at a Time

Bezos is famous (or perhaps infamous) for relentless attention to detail. He is reported to be fanatical about knowing, understanding, being involved in, and approving even the minutest detail about his business. Bezos unquestionably has vision. But he also has a total commitment to execution. No detail is too small to escape his view.

Although the "experts" criticize him, Bezos refuses to give up operational control of his business. There can be no question that there is a limit to the detail that can be driven by even the most industrious and committed manager—and Bezos surely must be reaching that limit. But he makes no excuses about the fact that his job is as much about execution as it is about vision.

As it turns out, Bezos's vision and execution skills pioneered a new way for consumers of buying not just books but CDs, DVD, videos, apparel, and other categories of consumer items. It might be said that Amazon created a new way of consuming that paved the way for eBay and many other online retailers. While the jury may still be out on the long-term viability prospects for his company, there can be no question that Bezos changed the world forever.

Dell: Rewriting the World's Job Description

Michael Dell disproved the old business axiom that it pays to be first (business school professors call the theory "the first market mover"). Dell Computer, the "last in" PC manufacturer, changed not just the computer industry, but people's jobs as well. From his dorm room at the University of Texas at Austin, Michael Dell conceived of a new way of making and selling personal computers. Taking on the industry giants like IBM, HP, Compaq, and Apple, he pioneered a new "supply and customer chain" concept that brought the cost of a computer to within the reach of billions of people around the planet.

As a result of his efforts, the PC industry was totally restructured and began to rapidly reduce prices to meet the new Dell standard. Several of his competitors were merged, consolidated, or sold (e.g., Digital Equipment into Compaq, then Compaq into HP; IBM sold to the Chinese computer company Lenovo). Now the largest computer company in the world, Dell sells more than $50 billion worth of PCs and related equipment a year. More importantly, Michael Dell has almost single-handedly changed the world's job description by making a reasonably priced computer affordable to almost everyone. Today, virtually every productive worker in the world—in the office, the factory, or even on a farm—is totally reliant on a PC.

Michael Dell and Jeff Bezos are just two examples of pioneers who have changed their industry and our lives. Herb Kelleher (Southwest Airlines), Howard Schultz (Starbucks), and Bill Gates (Microsoft) could be added to the list as well. What's the common thread? Brilliant vision followed by committed, untiring, even maniacal, flawless execution. Master P may not be tightly focused on one industry as Gates or Kelleher, but he uses the same relentless commitment for success.

Brilliant Vision; Flawless Execution

Since sometime in the early 1980s, the term "vision" has been a watchword of business. Every business needed one and most got them, ready or not. At times it seemed that business competition was only about vision. Who had the biggest, boldest, slickest, and most inspiring vision? Even President George H. W. Bush often referred to "the vision thing."

One of the first business leaders to break with "the vision thing" came in 1993 when Lou Gerstner took over IBM, with the mandate to right a company that was badly faltering. In just weeks after his appointment, reporters and financial analysts were bugging him almost daily about his vision for IBM. After some reflection, he responded rather abruptly, saying that IBM already had a vision, what they needed was better execution.

Echoing Gerstner's sentiments, Ram Charan and Larry Bossidy (former CEO of Honeywell International), in their best-selling book, *Execution: The Discipline of Getting Things Done*, suggest that execution is "the missing link between aspirations and results." Their conclusion: "Leaders don't focus nearly enough on follow-through, on actually getting things done."

Charan, a former GE executive and one of the most sought-after consultants in the world, says, "A leader cannot issue edicts from a mountaintop and expect to get things done, nor can he or she only be a 'big picture' thinker. Those at the top must be deeply involved in three areas: picking other leaders, setting the strategic direction, and conducting operations. These things cannot be delegated, no matter what the size of the organization."

Master P: No Limit to the Details

Percy Miller named his organization No Limit to express his vision that the enterprise had a limitless future. It could just as easily have referred to his attention to detail: no limits.

Simmons, Jay-Z, Dash, Diddy, 50 Cent, Eminem, and others

exhibit an almost pathological attention to key details of their image and commitment to overseeing the execution of every aspect of their businesses. But no one spots an opportunity and immediately moves on it better or more intently than Master P. He is fanatical about seeing projects through, and in a way that enriches the bottom line. Perhaps it's because Master P, more than any of the others, has his own money at stake.

Jeff Clanagan, CEO of Code Black Entertainment, ran Miller's film production company, No Limit Films, in the late 1990s. He says, "The difference between Master P and everyone else is that Master P was never afraid to invest his own money in himself. When he wanted to do something, he did it. Unlike many other so-called moguls, he always owned 100 percent of his company. He is one of the most pure entrepreneurs out there."

From Dixieland to Gangsta Land

Master P was born Percy Miller, in 1969, in New Orleans. His birthplace is a city with a rich musical history, but plenty of violent crime. He grew up in the Calliope projects, possibly the most crime-ridden part of a crime-ridden city. He managed to stay out of any big trouble, however, and spent much of his youth being a normal kid and playing a lot of basketball.

When his parents divorced, his mother moved to California, leaving little Percy going back and forth a lot between there and Louisiana. He became a high school star on the basketball court and won a scholarship to the University of Houston. He dropped out long before finishing, though, and moved to where his mother lived, studying business at a local community college.

At the end of the 1980s, his grandfather died and left Percy ten thousand dollars. Most of his friends probably would have spent it in a heartbeat, buying flashy clothes, rims, jewelry, or drugs. As he would prove so often later in life, however, Percy Miller knew an opportunity when he saw it. He took the ten thousand dollars and opened a small music store in Richmond, California, north of Oakland, stocking it with the "street buzz" rap he knew would sell in his neighborhood.

After a while, Miller learned that there was a limit to his inventory, however. Buyers were disappointed with a lot of rap that the major labels were cranking out. Few companies were putting out the kind of raw, funky beats that were the most popular in his city, where most of the residents were either black or Latino.

In 1990 Miller started distributing some neighborhood recordings and began making a modest amount of money meeting neighborhood demand. When he wanted to expand his sales base, he did it the old-fashioned way, booming music out of his car in the parking lots of rap concerts and selling CDs and cassettes out of the trunk. A few records caught on in a wider area, however, generating bona fide regional hits. Several songs were included on a compilation album, *West Coast Bad Boyz*, that spent months on the top album chart.

Percy Miller, now Master P, knew he was onto something. He left the store, moved the record label to New Orleans, and dived in full force.

No Limit's Unlimited Success: Flawless Execution

Much of Miller's success came from having a keen sense of the bottom line. On the West Coast, he had gotten his start making something out of nothing, turning cheaply recorded rap music into underground hits. After moving No Limit to his hometown of New Orleans, he quickly cranked up the production line and became the undisputed hip-hop master of execution—brilliant execution!

He and his team of producers, Beats by the Pound, worked on every release. They crafted the sound, designed the garish covers, and kept the process moving along quickly. A few albums reportedly went from recording studio to the street in two weeks flat. "The big joke among people that worked for Master P when I was there," says Jeff Clanagan, "is that nobody ever saw him sleep. He would call at 2:30 in the morning to talk business."

Master P learned a lesson and applied it from the start: keep costs low, spread the risks, and make money quickly. He has never been interested in the big-budget showpiece album, accompanied by star producers, expensive guests, and high-budget videos. He recorded quickly and on the cheap. He signed hungry young acts who were in a hurry to get their music out. Half the time the artists were family members. Album covers looked like something thrown together at a kitchen table. The CDs often contained twenty songs and never sold at a premium price point.

And it worked, time after time. For many releases the bills were paid the week the CDs shipped. All the rest was profit. He says he took lessons from the military background of his grandfather and always thought of the company as a unit. One soldier wouldn't cut it—the unit needed a whole army of soldiers. When one wasn't at his peak, the others would make up for it.

The strategy paid off and the profits were plentiful. By most critics' accounts, Master P wasn't much of a rapper. Apart from his eventual signing of Snoop Dogg, neither were most of the acts on his roster during the label's heyday. No Limit's recordings were derided as musically unimaginative, cheap sounding, and interchangeable with one another. But the fans didn't care.

To date, Percy Miller has garnered an impressive twelve multi-platinum, ten platinum, and thirteen gold albums. In 1997 his *Ghetto D* album toppled one of Puff Daddy's to grab the number one spot on the album sales chart. Meanwhile, his stable of hard-core rappers—C-Murder, Silkk the Shocker, Mystikal, and his own group, Tru—turned cheaply recorded, stripped-down rap albums into sales monsters.

Flirting with the Suits

Rap music sales increased 51 percent in just a three-year period between 1995 and 1998, with 62 million rap albums sold in

1997 alone. With the increased success came a fountain of bad publicity.

Toward the end of the 1990s, the major labels were shying away from gangsta rap to avoid controversy. Into the void stepped Master P, giving the people what they still wanted: hard beats and hard lyrics, with no holding back. As Death Row Records started to collapse under Suge Knight's weight, Miller snapped up Snoop Dogg, adding star power to his label's roster of home-grown talent.

Like much gangsta rap, at least half of No Limit's sales were to white kids in the suburbs. As Gregor and Dimitri Ehrlich said in the book *Move the Crowd: Voices and Faces of the Hip-Hop Nation,* "If your mom grew up on Bob Dylan and your hormones are urging you into adolescent rebellion, cranking Tom Petty isn't quite going to shock her. Master P, with his gold-plated tank rolling onto a basketball court, has a little more voltage."

The 1996 Telecommunications Act threw a wrench into the music business. Radio owners, especially Clear Channel, went on a buying binge and started standardizing play lists. Music video channels were all becoming cogs in big corporate wheels. Seeing the writing on the wall in the new decade, Miller signed a straight distribution deal with Universal in 2001 and changed the name of his label to New No Limit.

In 2002 Miller's worth was estimated at $294 million, a decline from the peak, but still enviable. The Universal relationship didn't last long, however, and the two parted ways at the end of 2003. Miller found himself without a distributor for an album already in the can and signed up with independent Koch Records.

Recently, New No Limit albums released through Koch have been charting, but showing up in the middle of the pack instead of at the top. With a much tighter retail and media environment than in the 1990s, a big street hit is harder to come by. At the same time, his brother and former Tru group member, "C-Murder," is serving a life sentence in the Louisiana State Penitentiary after living out the gangsta life he rapped about. (Much to the chagrin of prison officials, he still somehow managed to record a whole album *and* shoot a video from inside the prison.)

Still, moving ten- to twenty thousand units a week does more for Master P's bottom line than it does for a conglomerate such as Time-Warner or Sony. With low production costs and a tight control on the marketing budget, it doesn't take a number one smash to get a CD release into the black. Besides, he knows the future of his label is all in his own hands and nobody else's. As he told *The Source* after the release of his album *Ghetto Bill*, "I got to go do my own thing. I got to get out here and create my own camp."

Hustling on the Streets and on the Court

Miller is a hustler, though, and proud of it, so he never looked at music as the only business to be in. He tells anyone who will listen

 ### "It Ain't Always About the Money"

In the aftermath of Hurricane Katrina in late August 2005, many hip-hop luminaries rushed to help the relief effort. Jay-Z and Diddy each donated one million dollars. Others pledged money and began plans for various concert fundraisers.

Reuters/*Billboard* reported that many in the music industry were rallying support for survivors. Among those leading the effort were Tim McGraw, Harry Connick Jr., and Wynton Marsalis. One of the most prominent, though, was Master P, who created the organization Team Rescue (teamrescueone.com) to get supplies to those left in New Orleans. He told reporters: "It ain't about No Limit or Cash Money. It's about New Orleans. We'll do whatever we have to do for our people."

Master P, who lost a home in the flood, reportedly put aside competition with other New Orleans–based hip-hop artists and planned a fund-raising tour with Cash Money—a rival label—and the artist Juvenile.

that he is not the best rapper around, but he is "the best hustler in the game." While his No Limit label was ringing like a cash register, Miller branched out into a dozen other directions. He had a hand in recording studios, films, restaurants, a chain of shoe stores, a toy business, and even a phone-sex operation—whatever was a clearly profitable business with little risk. In one strange twist, Miller ended up negotiating the NFL contract of Heisman Trophy winner Ricky Williams, who became an up-and-down figure with the Miami Dolphins. Some projects failed and were quickly dropped. Overall, though, the other ventures added to the bottom line and added some stability when gangsta rap's popularity started to wane.

Master P may have beat out Chicago Bulls legend Michael Jordan on that 1999 *Fortune* list of wealthy young men—Jordan came in one spot behind—but Miller has chased his basketball dream as hard as he has chased the music one. He trained with the Charlotte Hornets, but was cut in training camp in 1998. He had also tried out for the Denver Nuggets and Toronto Raptors, but missed the final cut each time. He went on to play for several teams in the minor-league ABA (American Basketball Association), however, and played for the Sacramento Kings' summer league.

At the same time, he has won respect as a coach. In July 2005 he took a team of kids in the under-fifteen class to the AAU (Amateur Athletic Union) national championship—and won. Even better, both he and his son will probably make some cash out of it. The year before, Nickelodeon filmed the team's training and move through the tournament for TEENick.

From Father to Son

Master P's son Romeo Miller, better known as Lil' Romeo, is already a popular actor on Nickelodeon, after first becoming a platinum-selling rapper at the ripe age of eleven. His first single, "My Baby," went all the way to number one on the *Billboard* Hot

100 Singles chart. "My Baby" earned him 2001 Billboard Music Awards for rap artist of the year and rap single of the year.

When father Percy Miller approached Nickelodeon with the idea for a family sitcom starring his young son, it turned out to be a great match. Nickelodeon was looking for diversity to attract a wider audience of kids, and Master P had already proven his acting chops in movies. With Miller backing the project as executive producer, it was a good deal all around and a deal that has paid off well for both parties. After it launched in 2003, *Romeo!* received the best ratings in the network's history for a Saturday nighttime slot. According to Nielsen research, the show typically ranks in the top five each week across all networks in the kids aged 9 to 14 category and in the top twenty among teens aged 12 to 17. Romeo himself won an award as Favorite TV Actor in the Nickelodeon 2005 Kid's Choice Awards show. The show even got a thumbs-up from Common Sense Media, a nonpartisan, nonprofit organization that bills itself as "Your Family Friendly Entertainment Guide."

The clean image extends to Romeo and his raps, with lyrics that have nothing in common with the thug songs No Limit became famous for. Lil' Romeo's songs are closer to the late '90s Puff Daddy: sample an old hit, add some new raps, and mix it right for the radio. Leave it to Master P to once again spot an opening and jump on it. Just as his own solo career and label looked to be declining at the beginning of this decade, his son's career took off. As Jason Birchmeier wrote in a Romeo bio for Yahoo Music, "Suddenly, Master P seemed relevant once again, thanks to his son, with an album that didn't even warrant a parental advisory sticker; once again proving that even if the Southern entrepreneur's reputation had been built through exploitation rather than aesthetics, he was surely one of rap's craftiest businessmen."

Romeo, now hitting sixteen, has already been in a few movies. The films have been forgettable so far, but his ongoing TV success could lead to plenty more roles in the future.

Clothing and the Movies

Master P calls their Nickelodeon show *Romeo!* a "modern-day *Partridge Family.*" Of course the Partridge family didn't have a clothing line to hawk. Miller has even started his son Romeo off on the entrepreneurial road with a line of sportswear, P. Miller Shorties. On the show Master P wears his P. Miller Signature Collection clothing, while his son wears P. Miller Shorties. And since the star is an aspiring young rapper hoping to make it big, he gets to perform on every episode, plugging his albums along the way. It all ties up in a nice package, with each piece reinforcing the other. Like many of Miller's ventures, his clothing line is low key. It is not getting headlines on the runways or turning heads in magazine ads. It's just another product line that makes some cash.

In mid-2005, Miller inked a multimillion-dollar deal with Asanti, the nation's top automobile wheel and rim designer. Tapping into a natural street culture tie-in, Miller's designs go beyond the standard of what has been available and puts as much bling on the car wheels as rappers wear on their fingers and chests. In typical hustler form, one of his latest singles, "I Need Dubs," is an ode to cars, with a very obvious plug for his new line of wheel rims. This follows an earlier deal with Bazooka audio, where Miller introduced a line of amplifiers and speakers for booming cars. Other projects are always in the works: a luxury watch line, energy drinks, and whatever else can be easily monetized along the way.

Quite a few rap stars have crossed over to a movie or TV career. Some, such as Queen Latifah, Ice-T, and Ice Cube, have made more money acting than they did rapping. Miller has seldom been a marquis name on movie posters, but he has had a long string of work in Hollywood. He has appeared in more than a dozen studio releases, such as *Gone in 60 Seconds* with Nicholas Cage and Angelina Jolie, *Undisputed* with Wesley Snipes, and

Hollywood Homicide with Harrison Ford. He made an appearance as himself in *Scary Movie 3*, which grossed $110 million at the box office in the United States.

He has also been busy behind the camera. He wrote and directed a half dozen movies and financed eight as producer. *I'm Bout It*, a raw, self-produced film about his life in the New Orleans ghetto, was a straight-to-video release, but that didn't keep it from being a big moneymaker.

Jeff Clanagan set up and ran Miller's film production company after working on some of Master P's music videos. "At the time, although he was fairly successful, the big studios had no idea who Master P was," says Clanagan. "So we said, 'Forget it—let's go direct.' Nobody was really doing direct to video at the time; it was mainly a rental market." No Limit Films put out the movie *I'm Bout It* in 1997 and sold close to five hundred thousand units—a record at the time. "It showed us that the audience would come to the product if you got it out there and marketed it correctly," Clanagan adds. "In two and a half years, we did $44 million in revenue from home video."

Master P told MTV news in 2002, "You gotta have plans. You gotta organize yourself for growing and that's what I did." After turning ten thousand dollars and lots of hustle into a fortune in the hundreds of millions, it looks like the growth plans worked out well.

Like his contemporaries featured in this book, what is most striking about Master P is his confidence that he can do almost anything he sets out to do. In 2003 he told PBS's Tavis Smiley that there was one thing he still needed to accomplish in his life: learn how to play golf.

Master P may have been the first southern rap entrepreneur to make the pages of *Forbes* and *Fortune*, but others have made plenty of bucks and a few are following closely in his footsteps.

9

DASH AND CARTER

Takin' Over the World

Jay-Z, Roc-A-Fella yo, know the name
I ain't a player get it right, I'm controllin the game
—JAY-Z
"The City Is Mine," from *In My Lifetime, Vol. 1*

Takin' Over the World: Makin' a Dash For It

When the average entrepreneur hits a net worth of nine figures
before the age of thirty-five, he or she might slow down a bit. Not
the aptly named Mr. Dash. Damon Dash.

With Kareem "Biggs" Burke and Shawn "Jay-Z" Carter, Dash
built the Roc-A-Fella entertainment and clothing empire, with a
drive that makes the average entrepreneur look downright lazy.
On more than one occasion he has said he wants what everybody
around him has, and then some. "I'm never trying to be a big fish
in a little pond. I wanna be a big fish in the ocean. I'm trying to
take over the whole world."

Raised in East Harlem by a single mother who worked as a
secretary, Dash has been a hustler since he bounced in and out of
private prep schools on scholarships. Multitasking from the start,
he hosted parties in Harlem in the early 1990s while starting a
music management business. He didn't have the talent to be a rapper himself, but he knew if he found a good artist he could make
that person a star, and make them both rich in the process.

When Dash found Shawn Carter, a former drug dealer and KFC cashier now known as Jay-Z, he used the money he made at parties to finance Jay-Z's recording career. When Dash couldn't land a record deal for his artist, he employed his instinctive hustling skills, selling CDs out of his car and pushing DJs at radio and clubs to play the singles.

Eventually Dash and Carter got the attention of Priority Records, who ventured with the young entrepreneurs to release Jay-Z's commercial debut, *Reasonable Doubt*. That album eventually went gold at the end of the '90s, then platinum in the early 2000s, selling more than a million copies. After Jay-Z recorded a duet with female rapper Foxy Brown, her label, Russell Simmons's Def Jam, got interested in Dash and his company. They formed a fifty-fifty joint venture that turned out to be a financial bonanza for both companies over a ten-year period.

The New King of New York Rap

In 1998 Jay-Z's *Hard Knock Life* album debuted at number one on the *Billboard* 200 Albums chart and stayed there for five weeks. The album sold three million copies that year and eventually more than six million copies. By the late 1990s Roc-A-Fella was raking in about $50 million in annual revenues, much of it from Jay-Z's unparalleled success. The 1999 follow-up, *Life and Times of S. Carter,* was another number one debut and sold several million copies.

Jay-Z became the undisputed king of rap in New York, taking the throne from the deceased Biggie Smalls. Success continued into the next decade. His 2001 release, *The Blueprint,* also debuted at number one and sold 450,000 copies in its first week, despite coming out the week of the 9/11 terrorist attacks. He also became the first nonathlete to have a signature line of sneakers, through Reebok. Any doubts about whether kids playing basketball would buy a sneaker endorsed by a rapper were quickly dispelled. These shoes set a new record for the fastest-selling Reebok shoe in history.

The joint venture between Roc-A-Fella and Def Jam eventually yielded ten platinum albums, and Jay-Z became a veritable franchise, bringing a Midas touch to every project he guest-starred on. He teamed up with R. Kelly for two R&B albums and with Linkin' Park for a "mash up" rock album. Despite the oddness of the latter effort, the album was yet another number one debut. All the while he sold millions of his own CDs each year.

Cross-Promotions: Cashing In on the Franchise

The trio of Dash, Jay-Z, and Briggs ventured into other businesses while trying to find ways to wring more money from their existing enterprises. Things really came together in 1999, when Dash set out to wage a grand scale hip-hop arena tour dubbed the "Hard Knock Life Tour." The tour was a blistering success, a fifty-four-city sell-out, bringing in heaps of cash for the artists, including Jay-Z, other Roc-A-Fella acts, and the promoters.

But Dash was frustrated with the music industry's low margins and the need to split revenue into so many buckets. The natural next step, in his eyes, was starting up a clothing business. After all, Jay-Z could launch a successful clothing style just by wearing it in concert or, even better, wearing it in music videos seen by millions. If he mentioned the clothing in a song, too, the promotion would last even longer. Every time the video aired on TV or the song aired on the radio, it was money in the bank, with no need to worry about a royalty split between songwriter, producer, artist, and record label.

Rocawear was an immediate success, pulling in close to $20 million in gross revenue its first year, and by eighteen months, $80 million. Damon signed up models such as Victoria Beckham and Naomi Campbell, but the best celebrity was built into the deal: as soon as Jay-Z wore the clothes in videos, they flew off the shelves. Soon the other Roc-A-Fella artists were wearing them for videos and concerts.

"Getting Paid for What We Promote"

After the success of Rocawear, Dash started to take on complementary companies, including movie and video production, a vodka company, a magazine, and sneakers, and promoting them together wherever possible. Marketers call it "cross-promotion," or sometimes simply, "synergy." What Dash called it, though, was "getting paid for what we promote."

In the past few years, Dash has added a European cable TV channel, a beverage business, and a boxing promotions company. Was all this diversification risky? Dash saw it as the opposite: diversifying away from the risky music business. Recently he's bankrolled a platinum-edged hip-hop lifestyle magazine called, simply, *America*.

In 2004 Damon Dash raised plenty of eyebrows by revealing that Roc-A-Fella had purchased the Pro-Keds Sneaker Company, a footwear staple that was founded in 1949. A known sneaker nut, Dash saw it as another natural move. He loved the product and believed he could do a better job of marketing it than the current owners were doing.

One of his first moves was releasing a limited edition Pro-Keds sneaker to mark the tenth anniversary of the Roc-A-Fella brand. Only twenty-five hundred pairs were created, and each one was fully accessorized with a tenth-year string bag and a Roc-A-Fella CD. Naturally, the special sneakers sold out quickly and created an extra media buzz for the whole empire.

The New Boss: The King Becomes CEO

In 2004 Kanye West's debut album exploded onto the charts and sold more than three million copies, adding a second star to the

America **the Beautiful**

The one cultural media that hip-hop hasn't truly conquered, at least from within the magic circle of the moguls, is magazines. A couple of independent magazines have made a real success out of covering the genre, such as *The Source* and *Vibe*. Over the years others existed on the outside of the genre, barely holding on, or eventually folding (*Elemental, Fatlace, Mass Appeal, Scratch, Tablist, and Waxpoetics*). Some of the moguls have even tried and failed with their own entrants, like Russell Simmons's *One World*. But that doesn't stop them from trying. Two new entrants are *Shade 45* from Eminem, and *America* financed by Damon Dash.

America is a truly beautiful publication with lush photos from some of the world's top photographers. Its edges are trimmed in platinum. Aimed at the aspirations and accomplishments of the hip-hop lifestyle, *America* (despite its name) follows in the spirit of European glossies that are seldom seen on U.S. shelves. *America* is trendy, smart, cool, and hip. And Damon is not visibly present. Says founder and editor/publisher Smokey Fontaine:

> Damon gives us full autonomy to run the magazine. He looks to me to run this publication with the same set of skills that make him a great CEO. These skills can't be bought. You have to be clear-eyed in recognizing your strengths and weaknesses and surround yourself with great people that can do their jobs better than you.
>
> Damon is a brilliant businessman and a charismatic personality. But he is not in business to be loved by everyone, because at the end of the day, like any other CEO, he needs results.
>
> *America* is not a puff piece to promote Damon. Its goal is to honestly and accurately reflect, in the highest quality way, the hip-hop community. It is a business, but it's a magazine with a mission. Damon's lived up to every commitment he's made to us.

roster. But Island Def Jam, Roc-A-Fella's parent music company, exercised their right to buy the remaining 50 percent of the company for $10 million, a real bargain considering the catalog titles and an ascending Kanye West. At that point, the company's annual revenues had hit $65 million.

Dash agreed to continue working with Roc-A-Fella and Def Jam as a consultant, but quickly founded the Damon Dash Music Group as a new venture with the same company. L. A. Reid, the chairman of Island Def Jam Music Group, said when announcing the formation of Damon Dash Music Group, "The popularization and mainstreaming of rap and hip-hop into the pop world owes a monumental debt to the vision and courage that Roc-A-Fella put forward on behalf of its roster of artists."

When the sale was announced, Jay-Z was named president and CEO of Def Jam, a move so unexpected that it made feature story news in national business publications. Suddenly the artist was the executive and the executive was looking for a new start. And after an upward career trajectory that rarely slowed over a ten-year period, Dash was suddenly faced with reshuffling and revamping his empire.

From Blink to Bling

Kenny Burns of clothing company RyanKenny was vice president at Roc-A-Fella right up to the split, running the R&B side and helping Dash get the film business going. "That partnership between Damon and Jay-Z is at an end, but so what?" he says. "When you think that these guys made $500 million dollars together, who's mad? . . . They are grown men who made a lot of money together and made a difference for a lot of people, with all kinds of jobs and opportunities." Nobody needs to worry about whether Dash will keep spawning companies or not, says Burns. "Damon has a great mind and really applies himself 100 percent to everything he does. He will continue to be successful wherever he goes, whatever he does."

What separates Dash from many other businesspeople is his ability to seize the moment, to know almost instantly what will work and what won't. The instinct is so powerful, yet mysterious, that most businesspeople don't like to talk about it, at least not in public. Behind closed doors, when the boardroom discussion is away for prying ears, they'll call it "instinct," or more descriptively, "gut feel," or "tummy judgment." Instinct has only rarely made the business press, or management how-to books, as a legitimate business decision-making tool. That is, until author Malcolm Gladwell popularized the notion with the best-selling book *Blink: The Power of Thinking Without Thinking*.

The power of *thinking without thinking* is what sets Dash apart from the other moguls. He has the uncanny ability to see things quickly, size them up accurately, and make decisions with what his associates call the "supreme confidence" to do what he needs to do and never look back. As the accompanying sidebar demonstrates, he's the master at going from blink to bling.

With a shrug, Dash announced in mid-2005 that he was walking away from the Rocawear clothing line after his current design obligations were done. He'll concentrate on his own homegrown clothing launches—State Property, Team Roc, and the Dame Dash collection. He told MTV, "I'm a businessman; I have no emotional attachments to any of my businesses. I'm a hustla, I flip things."

The Damon Dash Keys to Success

While some rap moguls are coy about how they make their money, Dash is proud to be a hustler, an entrepreneur, and a tycoon. He keeps no secrets when it comes to outlining the reasons for his success.

GO AT IT HARD.

Even in his youth, Damon Dash was continually trying to find new ways to make a buck, and he bragged to anyone who would listen that he was going to be a business tycoon someday. He

◐ Dash: "Supreme Confidence" in His Convictions

Malcolm Gladwell made a big impression in business circles with his now-classic book *The Tipping Point: How Little Things Can Make a Big Difference.* It captured business' attention with its idea that certain things accelerate dramatically after reaching a critical level. Hip-hop could be said to have reached the tipping point sometime in the late 1990s.

Gladwell followed up that book with *Blink: The Art of Thinking Without Thinking.* It is having an equally serious effect on business thinking. The biggest impact is that it is bringing "instinct" out of the closet and into the everyday discussions of business. It has, in effect, legitimized "tummy judgment."

Acceptance isn't automatic, though. As Gladwell says, "We are innately suspicious of this kind of rapid cognition. We live in a world that assumes that the quality of a decision is directly related to the time and effort that went into making it . . . we ask [doctors] for a second opinion . . . What do we tell our children? Haste makes waste. Look before you leap. Stop and *think.* Don't judge a book by its cover."

But *Blink* documents its case well. After much research in many fields of endeavor, Gladwell declares, "The simple fact: decisions made quickly can be every bit as good as decisions made cautiously and deliberately."

To be sure, Gladwell points out that not every quick decision is right, just as the slow ones aren't always right either. What's important, he says, is the skill, experience, and innate gift that some people possess to get it right quickly. They feel it in their tummy.

Dash Damon has demonstrated conclusively that he has a great feel for the hip-hop cultural market. He knows in his tummy what will work and what won't. And then he combines the second critical ingredient for success: the *supreme confidence* to trust his gut.

What sets Dash apart is that he *gets it* and he *gets it quickly.* Some might say in a blink.

put unbridled energy into his party promotion business, and it was this drive and energy that most impressed the young Shawn Carter, soon to be the star Jay-Z.

Although he would be loath to admit it, Dash shares a lot of similarities with Sean "Diddy" Combs in this respect. Both men grew up saying they were going to get rich, both grabbed any opportunity that came along to get there, and both continually put the need to sleep at the very bottom of their priority list. Of course while Diddy loves to be a star in the spotlight, Dash is more content to work the machinery and watch the money roll in.

Dash doesn't see having five or six jobs as a strain. In an interview with MSNBC he said, "If someone has five or six kids, they can raise their five or six kids; it's just proper time delegation and knowing how to delegate your attention. I just don't sleep, really, know what I mean?"

In the spring of 2005, one of Dash's artists, Beanie Sigel, was behind bars in the state pen when his second album came out. With his star in the slammer, Dash took on the challenge of publicizing the album himself. He did whirlwind interview tours with the print media and visited radio stations. The result: the album debuted at number three on the *Billboard* pop album chart, selling more than 130,000 copies at retail. It was featured in major newspapers, including the *Los Angeles Times* and *New York Times*. Dash filmed a documentary that ran in its entirety on BET, MTV, and other channels. At the same time, he was promoting his *State Property 2* movie, which starred Sigel (filmed prior to the prison sentencing).

DIVERSIFY AND CROSS-PROMOTE RELIGIOUSLY.
"How can we make more money from Jay-Z's success?" This was the question bugging Dash in the late 1990s. So he and the team came up with some answers. They started a clothing line and had Jay-Z wear the clothes and talk about them in all of his other ventures.

He has not shied away from using each of these vehicles to

promote the other. Nearly every frame of the film *State Property 2* shows off the products of his commercial empire. Not only do the characters wear State Property jackets, T-shirts, and caps, but they also seem to drink only Armadale vodka, Dash's premium brand, and wear clothes from his Rocawear line, including Pro-Keds sneakers. It's a Damon Dash promo vehicle as well: he is listed as director, cowriter, producer, and, oh yes, lead actor. Dash is producing an *Apprentice*-style show for BET called *The Ultimate Hustler.* Entrepreneurial contestants compete for a spot working for Dash's empire.

Is it all too much for one man, even Dash? As *Fortune* questioned: "Most entrepreneurs find it challenging to run one business they know well, never mind a dozen in new and highly competitive fields. Does Dash have the management skills to coordinate such seemingly incongruous businesses as jewelry, magazine publishing, boxing, and filmmaking?"

But *Fortune* forgot the sneakers, liquor, and . . . electronics. Yes, Dash recently released a line of MP3 players. So the answer to *Fortune*, of course, is yes—that is, where Damon Dash is concerned.

UNDERSTAND YOUR MARKET INTIMATELY.
In interviews, Dash is fond of saying, "I can sell anything I understand." As he told the U.K. newspaper *The Guardian*, he is good at fitting in with different crowds. "I'm comfortable in very extreme situations. I can go into the depths of the 'hood with the roughest type of guys and feel 100 percent comfortable, because I lived through it, survived it, and felt comfortable with it. I'm also confident I can go into the boardroom with non-urban people and feel 100 percent comfortable, because I have lived the non-urban life at times and I survived it. I can relate and I can also translate."

Dash feels that many business owners have a serious disconnect with the culture of people they are trying to sell to. In some ways this has been traditional in the music business, with middle-aged family men (and later women) making decisions on what teenagers are going to buy. "But if you want to sell to a certain demographic, you have to understand it. The majority of big corporations don't."

INVEST IN YOUR PEOPLE
AND THEN LET THEM PERFORM.

Becoming part of the Damon Dash empire requires more than a strong interview performance. Even those joining his security entourage need to graduate from his "boot camp." As he explained to *The Guardian*, "When I want to employ somebody, I try to build them from A to Z. Before I put you in the field with one of my businesses, I would spend very intensive time with you to put you through the shit work so you appreciate the move up. You got to watch how I work and see what I expect from people. If you pass through boot camp, you can move on and get into my company."

Once they reach that point, Dash will often empower people and give them their own businesses to run. The new Damon Dash Music Group gives individual artists their own labels under one umbrella. The Roc-A-Fella film production company gives wide latitude to producers and directors. Dash Dibella Promotions, the sports management company, aims to give its stable of boxers a bigger than usual stake in their own success.

With artists and their music, Dash is far less of a control freak than he is with his business decisions. As he told VH-1, "It's their music. I'm capitalizing off them. All I can do is give advice. I never enforce, ever, to any of my artists."

OWN WHAT YOU PROMOTE.

When Damon Dash's music artists are promoting a brand in their songs or videos, he wants a piece of it. If he thinks he could be marketing the brand better than the owner is, he takes it into his own hands by buying the company. "I have a problem with making other people money," he told MSNBC.

Dash launched a jewelry business (his Tiret watches run from $17,000 to $130,000) after spending millions of dollars with bling king "Jacob the Jeweler" in New York City. He bought Anandale vodka after realizing his artists were helping the company make money by mentioning it in songs, but were not getting anything out of it.

Not surprisingly, the biggest impact has been in fashion, where the style sense and promotional abilities of Dash and Jay-Z have led to a sizable clothing empire. (Rocawear battles with Sean Combs's Sean John company for bragging rights as the top-selling urban brand.)

MAKE HIGH-PERCENTAGE BETS.

As innovative and powerful as the Roc-A-Fella umbrella became, Dash's success on the Hollywood side could charitably be called "modest." In 1999, in conjunction with Dimension Films, Roc-A-Fella Films released *Backstage*, a behind-the-scenes documentary tracing the path of the Hard Knock Life tour. It didn't exactly break into the mainstream. In 2001 Roc-A-Fella Films released *State Property*, starring Roc-A-Fella rap artist Beanie Sigel, for Lion's Gate. It left theaters almost as quickly as it got there.

Dash directed and produced the independent comedy *Death of a Dynasty*, an odd satire about the world of hip-hop that fizzled with both critics and crowds. *Paid in Full* and *Paper Soldiers* followed, with neither film lighting up the box office. His credibility took an upward turn though when he produced *The Woodsman*, an indie film starring Kevin Bacon. The movie won awards at both Sundance and Cannes. Dash claims that based on these awards alone, the movie made a profit just from the licensing deals for foreign distribution and CDs.

While none of his films have been around very long in theaters, all were filmed with an eye on economics and were no-brainers in Dash's eyes. *State Property 2* reportedly only cost $2 million to make. That wouldn't even cover the catering bill for many Hollywood productions.

Time will tell if he needs to succumb to orthodox Hollywood economics to become a success in the film world. As this book was being written, Dash was finishing production on a film called *Shadowboxer,* starring Cuba Gooding Jr., Helen Mirren, and Macy Gray.

What About Jay?

When next decade's hip-hop moguls book is written, Shawn Jay-Z Carter will probably be in the thick of it. Although he was the front man instead of the back office man during much of his career, that all changed when he was named president and CEO of Def Jam.

He certainly didn't accept the job for the salary. In *Fortune* magazine's 2004 "America's 40 Richest People Under 40" issue, Jay-Z's wealth was estimated to be $286 million. He has so much money rolling in that he bought a stake in the New Jersey Nets basketball team. Why? Although he didn't say so at the time, you can be sure his answer would be, like the way he deals with the rest of the world: "Because I can!" He's done a lot to promote the team, including the recording of a playoff anthem when they headed to the NBA tournament in 2005.

Despite the public split with Damon Dash, the two are still working on a few lingering projects together, including a jewelry partnership with Lucas Design International (LDI). Nevertheless, Carter looks to be striking many of his own deals in the future. Public announcements have him soliciting offers for a new S. Carter line of men's formal wear. He has also launched a line of luxury watches with Audemars Piguet, with prices starting at $23,000.

As the head of Roc-A-Fella under Def Jam, one of his first moves was to establish a world music label, Roc La Familia. "Everybody talks about the world getting smaller—well, we are doing something about it," he announced. "Roc La Familia will leverage the extensive resources of Def Jam to introduce fans to cultures that they would not normally be exposed to." The new imprint will release work from genres like reggae, reggaeton, calypso, tribal, and West Indian.

As the newest kid on the entrepreneurial block, as the new boss in town, Jay-Z's legacy is yet to be written. It's too early to call. One thing is for sure, as the Sinatra theme song might say: "He'll do it his way."

10

EAST COAST—WEST COAST—GULF COAST

But Southern Rap?
Ludacris!

THE SOUTH. HOME of country music and NASCAR. Bubba and grits. But rap? Hip-hop? Y'all gotta be kiddin' me!

Country and hip-hop have shared the distinction of alternatively sharing the number one and two spots of top-selling music genres for a decade. Why? Perhaps because both speak to what's on the mind of the common man. Straight. Direct. Street talk. Heartfelt. Money. Love and heartache. No taboos. No mincin' words.

Success makes strange bedfellows, as the old saying goes. And it seems there's more in common between country and hip-hop than anyone would have thought. *USA Weekend* magazine figured it out with a special 2005 cover story featuring one of the biggest stars of country music—Toby Keith—and the reigning star of southern rap—Ludacris (Chris Bridges), for what they dubbed "a celebration of kindred musical spirits. [Country and rap] are rooted in real stories about real people . . . and are the most authentic American genres today."

Hip-hop and country music also share a common geographic root: the hills and valleys of the Old South. The Negro spiritual, born in the misery of the cotton field, is the direct lineal progenitor of jazz, soul, R&B, and ultimately hip-hop. Country music was born in the nearby hills, the songs of poor, illiterate sharecroppers and mountain dwellers. Country and hip-hop, and their cousins, jazz and rock, arguably hold the claim to be the only original, indigenous American musical forms.

Returning to Its Roots: Just a Beat Behind

Willie Nelson is one of country music's great stylists and one of its undisputed master wordsmiths (he penned such classics as "Crazy," "Blue Eyes," and "Always on My Mind"). A great solo performer as well, Willie's signature style was to sing just a half second behind the beat. So, too, it seems with southern rap.

Things do move slower in the South. It's hot, it's humid. Getting in too much of a hurry can wear a person out. So it was with rap in the South. While the East Coast and West Coast were having their beef, the South was quietly building up its rap scene, just a beat behind.

But the times have changed. Today, it's the New South. Up-to-date. Leading. Innovating. Trend-setting. In the new millennium, it's hard to imagine a time when southern rap wasn't hot. In Atlanta, Ludacris has racked up five albums that have sold two million or more copies. Even that pales in comparison to the success of OutKast, whose last album—a two-CD set—sold a staggering ten million copies. Virginia Beach has spawned Missy Elliott, the most consistently successful rap female, and the unstoppable producers Timbaland and the Neptunes.

Newer acts like the Ying Yang Twins are seeing platinum success out of the box. Houston rapper Slim Thug didn't even wait for the box to open. His major label debut was brashly titled *Already Platinum.*

It wasn't always this way. Regional hits were the norm from the 80s to the mid '90s, until Master P's label exploded and started hitting the upper regions of the sales charts. By the mid-2000s the South had more stars than New York or LA. In Atlanta—known in rap circles as "the ATL"—acts Lil Jon and OutKast are just the most visible success stories in that thriving city. Gold albums are popping out from artists in Memphis, Miami, Houston, and St.

Rap Music Regional Reach

Louis—and new acts are emerging from many places in between. In Louisiana, Master P's New No Limit and Bryan Williams's Cash Money are still active in New Orleans.

Luke Campbell Kicks It

The southern rap scene started out with more notoriety than respect. Miami-based Luther "Luke Skywalker" Campbell was in some ways the first southern rap mogul. His 2 Live Crew albums were independently produced outside the major label system and sold millions. Most of those sales were based on the novelty value, however, despite the Miami "deep bass" sound. The lyrics were shockingly crude, and the live shows featured props such as barely clothed strippers. Album covers featured women in thongs, and the videos rarely departed from the same script.

Legal troubles continually dogged the group. A record store owner was famously arrested for selling a copy to a minor, and another was arrested for selling a copy to an undercover cop after the album was banned in Florida's Broward Country. (Three years later, the U.S. Supreme Court overturned the obscenity ruling.)

The group was arrested on obscenity charges after one performance, but acquittal soon followed. Campbell wasn't so lucky with his assumed name though: Hollywood's George Lucas successfully sued to keep him from using the Luke Skywalker name.

After sales that peaked at two million with *As Nasty As They Wanna Be*, in 1989, 2 Live Crew faded into obscurity. Campbell made several comeback attempts, but eventually lost his brief fortune. Nevertheless, many later southern rap performers and businesspeople point to Campbell as the one who first opened the door. He showed that rap music didn't have to be from New York or California to succeed. Musically, much of the current "crunk music" of the South can be traced to Campbell's production style.

Fast Followers: Southern Hardballers

In business strategy terms, southern rap would be labeled "fast followers." Not the first, not the last, but expert at sensing the winning path as innovative leaders fight it out, then pouncing quickly when the results are near. A cop-out? Bad strategy? Second best? Not at all, if some of the world's biggest companies are any measure. Among the noted fast followers: GE, IBM, and Microsoft. The strategy in a nutshell: let the pioneers blaze a trail, then swoop in with the best solution and clean up!

First Market Movers?

One of business' great strategy myths is called "the first market mover." It argues that the first mover (the first entrant, first to change a technology, etc.) in a market gets the lion's share of the profits. So the idea has been adopted as gospel, and many businesspeople think if they're not first, why bother? The myth has proven right many times, but it's also proven wrong just as often. Thinking that first always wins makes no more sense than thinking that big is always better. WalMart is the biggest and the best retailer, but GM is the biggest but far from the best auto company. So what's the right answer?

The answer is that it's not as important *when* you enter a market as *what you do* when you get there. Some have made a tremendous amount of money being first: Sony with the Walkman, McDonald's with the fast-food chain, Apple with the iPod, and so forth. Many other companies have "cleaned up" as fast followers (being number two or three). Still others have been seventh or eighth or later and been the real winners. Southwest was one of the last entrants into the airlines industry. Dell was the same in computers. And there were plenty of coffee shops before Starbucks. The southern rappers are not the first, not the biggest, but in many ways they're making a run to be among the best.

Fast Followers!

The southern hip-hop entrepreneurs were a little later into the game, but have demonstrated they're hardball players, not willing to concede the market to the New Yorkers simply because they were first. Strategy consultant George Stalk, who described his hardball approach in chapter 2, says, "Softball competitors like to think their bright ideas are sacred. Hardball players know better. They're willing to take any good idea they see and use it to create competitive advantage for themselves. Some people might recoil when they're called a copycat. Hardball players couldn't care less."

Sirius Radio's Scott Lindy echoes Stalk when he says they've played it just right: "You can be just a nanosecond behind," he says, but "you strike when the iron's hot."

The Slow Rise of the South

Luther Campbell may have fanned the slow flame of rap in the South, but Georgia's Arrested Development struck while the iron was hot. And they couldn't be more different from 2 Live Crew.

The album united a mixed bunch of progressive thinkers and musicians who rapped about peace, love, family, and responsibility. The group's first single, "Tennessee," hit number one on the *Billboard* Rap/R&B Singles chart. Their debut album hit the top ten on the album chart, eventually selling several million copies. They won several Grammys and ended up on the top of most critics' year-end lists. They were never able to follow up this success on subsequent albums, but their brief fame was an inspiration to later successors such as OutKast and the Goodie Mob.

Houston's Hip-Hop Hotbed

Meanwhile, in Houston, Rap-a-Lot Records was creating a stir. James Smith formed Rap-a-Lot at the end of the 1980s and labored in relative obscurity until the Geto Boys started to catch on, along with later solo artist Brad "Scarface" Jordan. Like 2 Live Crew before them, they got plenty of publicity due to their offensive lyrics. In their case, however, it was due to extreme violence rather than sex. They depicted the violence and stark conditions in their Houston ghetto projects home and put everything they saw and thought on recordings—radio play and public opinion be damned. The songs often came off as the audio equivalent of a slasher flick. But founder Smith knew well that controversy would sell. Between 1991 and 1996 the Geto Boys reached platinum once and hit gold three times, all on Rap-a-Lot.

As a solo artist, Scarface ended up putting out four gold and three platinum albums from 1993 to 2000. His style of hard-boiled, ghetto-bred, hard-core rapping set the scene for many to come, and he became known as "the father of Southern thug rap." Appropriately enough, when Def Jam decided to set up a southern subsidiary, they tapped Scarface to be CEO. Seeing the South coming on strong in the early 2000s, Def Jam offered him a lucrative contract, the best industry connections, and a powerful marketing push. It first helped his own career, as 2002's *The Fix* became his best seller. The label also launched the career of Atlanta's Ludacris, who became a sensation. It then signed Shawnna and DTP and is currently building up its roster with other acts.

The Mass-Production Empires

When Percy "Master P" Miller started consistently putting southern hip-hop on the sales map in the mid '90s, it was a revelation. Over and over, his cheaply produced albums managed to give the people what they wanted—party songs and disposable rap they could crank up in the convertible. The beats were slower, the rhymes less complicated, the message street-real and seldom preachy.

The business plan for No Limit was all about keeping it in the family: more than half the artists at any given time were related. One production team handled the recording of every song. Everyone rapped on each other's albums, and the liner notes were blatant advertisements for coming releases by other acts. When the popularity of one act started to fade, others from the large stable were bound to be on the rise. Before No Limit, very few acts from the South went platinum. That all changed with Percy Miller's crew: Mystikal, Tru, Silkk the Shocker, C-Murder, and Master P himself quickly hit that level.

Of course the idea was easily duplicated. On Master P's turf of New Orleans, Cash Money Records had actually gotten an earlier start, with its first release in 1991. Things really took off for them in the late '90s, though, after Master P opened the doors. Cash Money went on to sell more than 25 million CDs worldwide since being started by Bryan "Birdman" Williams and his brother, Ronald "Slim" Williams. (Bryan Williams deserves special notoriety for supposedly coining the term "bling-bling" to describe the hip-hop habit of wearing pounds of shiny jewelry.)

The two brothers joined the ranks of rap multimillionaires after Universal Music came calling. Cash Money received $30 million of real cash money and was able to hold on to its masters. After the payout, however, many artists soon clashed with the label over their earnings, and there was a mass exodus of artists in 2001 over funds. Cash Money dwindled down to just two artists: Lil Wayne and the Big Tymers. The latter was Bryan Williams's own group, which had racked up five gold or platinum albums. Like a true "roll up the sleeves" entrepreneur, Bryan adopted the "Birdman" moniker and started rapping himself as a solo artist. He soon became the top artist on the label, releasing the gold-selling *#1 Stunna* album.

In 2003 former artist Juvenile returned to the label for one final album, an album that spawned a number one hit and was a smash success. Going to the negotiation table while the time was ripe, Bryan inked a new deal with Universal, reportedly for around $100 million. So far the Williams's empire has mainly been confined to music, though Bryan Williams did endorse a shoe line for Lugz and appeared in the movie *Beauty Shop*. In explaining the title of his 2005 album he said, "Throughout my life, I've had to do a little bit of everything just to survive. Some of the things I've done, I'm proud of and some I'm not, but in the end it was about getting paid, that's why I call this album *Fast Money*."

In Miami, Slip-n-Slide Records was trying to follow the same production line formula for success. Ted "Touche" Lucas founded Slip-N-Slide Records in 1994, but it took several years to break out. Their first three ventures were unabashed disasters. The first was a rap tour that got rained out. The second was an R&B album that was an instant flop. The third was another act who received the star treatment: big videos, a big recording budget, and lots of promotion. It flopped as well. The label finally hit commercial success with one of Ted's childhood friends, Trick Daddy, after much internal worry that he would end up in jail any day. MTV called him "One of the most thuggish rappers ever embraced by the mainstream."

The label owners took advantage of the Super Bowl being staged in Miami and worked the artist's second album hard all weekend.

By Monday morning they had a distribution deal signed with
Atlantic Records. At the turn of the decade, Trick Daddy's sales
took off based on several big club and radio hits. He ended up
with four platinum albums, including the latest release. A woman
named Trina guest-starred on his first album and then became
a star on her own. After a decade in the game, Slip-n-Slide has
sold more than nine million albums.

Atlanta: The Hip-Hop South

These days, rap stars are as likely to be from the South as not. In
some ways, Atlanta has become as much a hotbed of talent as New
York. Live venues are plentiful, a full industry infrastructure is in
place, and new labels are cranking out a wide range of artists. Lil
Jon is creating his own hip-hop empire with his own albums and
production duties. When he teams up with super producer Scott
Storch, the duo reportedly earns $150,000 per song. Now Lil Jon
has his own label on Warner Brothers—Black Market Entertainment—and an energy drink fittingly called "Crunk!!!"

The members of OutKast have wasted no time capitalizing on
the success of their last album. André Benjamin won raves for his
movie roles in *Be Cool* and *Four Brothers.* Both members starred
in an HBO movie together and supplied the soundtrack. Antwon
Andre Patton, better known as Big Boi, has his own music label,
Purple Ribbon, through Virgin. "The guys own a studio in Atlanta.
They own their own record label, started their own clothing line,"
says OutKast manager Michael "Blue" Williams. "Anything that
could create wealth for them, we tried to find a way to do."

So So Def: Jermaine Dupri

One of Atlanta's earliest moguls, Jermaine Dupri, started out
small—literally. He produced and managed the teenage rap duo
Kris Kross. After their album sold four million copies, he founded

the So So Def music label, releasing several successful adult acts and another child hit courtesy of Lil Bow Wow. The So So Def label became home to some twenty gold and platinum albums, including two of his own as a solo artist. He also did production work for such artists as TLC, Mariah Carey, Usher, and Janet Jackson.

In January 2005, around the time Jay-Z was named president of Def Jam, Dupri got the nod from Virgin Music. He was named president of Virgin's urban music division and, with his So So Def imprint thrown into the mix, the deal was estimated to come with a price tag of $20 million.

Dallas Austin: Getting As Big As Texas

No, Dallas Austin is not from Texas, but his talents are as big as that state. The Atlanta native's name is usually preceded by a bundle of titles, such as "producer/songwriter/keyboardist/remixer/studio owner." His musician and production credits could fill pages, running the gamut from Madonna to Aretha Franklin to Lenny Kravitz. Austin wrote and produced eight songs for the Boyz II Men debut album, *Cooleyhighharmony,* which sold more than ten million copies worldwide. Lately he's worked with Gwen Stefani, Nas, and even on a Duran Duran comeback album. Along the way he produced a slew of movie soundtracks, including those for *White Men Can't Jump* and Russell Simmons's remake of *The Nutty Professor.*

He owns a major recording studio in Atlanta and started a music label, Rowdy Records, by signing an unknown Atlanta singer named Monica. Her debut went multi-platinum, showing that Austin knew how to market as well as record. He also owns a film company, a merchandising and marketing company, and three music publishing companies. Who knows what he'll be able to accomplish now that he is in his thirties?

New-Wave Moguls

The founders of fashion company RyanKenny are prime examples of the next wave of moguls. Young, but experienced beyond their years, they are turning their nationwide connections into expanding empires. The business lines could make up a whole chaotic wall chart, with some lines based on personal relationships that lead to opportunities, some connected by pure cash flow. The three founders—Ryan Glover, Kenny Burns, and Derek Dudley—together and collectively touch fashion, jewelry, music publishing, record companies, artist management, a recording studio, event production, tequila, and more.

As cofounder Kenny Burns says, "To take over the throne, I have to know how the throne was built. I have studied it hard. Puffy, Russell, Andre, Damon—all of them are mentors to me. The thing about these guys is they show you the blueprint; they show you how to grow. I'm taking what the original moguls have shown me and I'm taking it to the next level."

Things might move a little slower in the South, but the southern hip-hop moguls aren't kicking back waiting for their turn. And they've become an integral part of the "Hip-Hop Nation."

11

HIP-HOP NATION

"What Else?"

Looking to take over the world is my goal
With my unstoppable crew takin' all control . . .

This is my planet, I'm bout business
The best that ever done it, can I get a witness?
(Uhhh!)

—LL COOL J
"Hit 'em High (The Monstar's Anthem),"
from the album *The DEFinition*, featuring B-Real

TO SAY HIP-HOP is going to take over the world is a stretch. To say hip-hop is a hit with mainstream Middle America is to understate the obvious. Hip-hop, along with country, dominates the music sales charts. Just how dominant is it? When rockers Green Day won the award for best artist at an MTV awards show, singer Billie Joe Williams said, "It's great to know that rock music still has a place at MTV."

But, armed with entrepreneurial instincts and unwavering drive, the moguls soon made rock and pop musicians like Aerosmith and Madonna look like relative paupers from a business standpoint. The moguls no longer worked for record companies—they owned them. From this musical base they soon expanded into other, often more profitable, businesses, where the margins were higher or more predictable and the consumers were more upscale.

Music, Yes, But "What Else?"

At the end of any new venture discussion with his staff or associates, Russell Simmons says it best when he asks: "What else?" It's Simmons's way of forcing people to think about, or search for, a product line extension, a new market, the next big opportunity, the next idea that will launch his enterprise in a new and profitable direction. "What else?" could easily be the anthem for the generation of hip-hop entrepreneurs who followed him. So, after the rhymes, "what else?"

Kanye West smiles out from the cover of *Time* magazine. LL Cool J is a guest on Ellen DeGeneres's midday talk show and sends Ellen's mostly white middle-class female audience into a frenzy as she helps him rip off his T-shirt. But LL broadly boasts in another venue that his first read every morning is the *Wall Street Journal.* Snoop Dogg is the featured star doing commercials for AOL, T-Mobile, and Chrysler (in the latter playing opposite Lee Iaccoca). Mattel now offers a line of hip-hop fashion Barbie dolls called "Flavas." Cruise any mall and you can count endless numbers of people wearing hip-hop-inspired clothing, many bearing the names Phat Farm, FUBU, or Sean John. The former Ice-T stars on one of America's favorite TV cop shows. And rappers are seemingly in every other action movie coming out of Hollywood.

Hip-hop now has so much power in the marketplace that one artist can influence fashion. The *Wall Street Journal* once reported that when Jay-Z said in a song, "I don't wear jerseys, I'm 30-plus," retail sales of NBA basketball jerseys immediately dropped off nationwide. Or, as successful designer Tommy Hilfiger told *USA Today Weekend* magazine, "Fashion is inspired by art, music, entertainment, movies, sports—and [America] is where it all happens. The music world has tremendous impact."

Hip-hop isn't going mainstream. Hip-hop *is* the mainstream. And no one is going mainstream faster than the former gangsta rapper turned entertainment everyman, Snoop Dogg. (See "Snoop Dogg: From Long Beach Gang Member to Celebrity Icon" below)

For several decades, rock music ruled. To be "a rock star"

Snoop Dogg:
From Long Beach Gang Member to Celebrity Icon

> If the ride is mo' fly
> You must buy!
> —SNOOP DOGG to Lee Iaccoca
> Chrysler TV Commercial

Calvin "Snoop Dogg" Broadushas has come a long way from being a scruffy kid with a weird voice doing some West Coast guest raps for Dr. Dre. His music has stayed popular for nearly fifteen years, with numerous gold and platinum albums. At this point, he could have just kicked back in the crib and collected the royalties.

Today, Snoop is everywhere. He hosts his own rap music show through XM satellite radio. He has appeared in more than ten movies, including *Training Day* and the remake of *Starsky and Hutch.* As this book was being completed, he was wrapping up production on the first entry of a horror film franchise called Snoop Dogg's *Hood of Horror.* Along the way, he became an unlikely fashion icon, culminating in his being recognized as "best dressed" at the 2005 MTV Video Music Awards show. Naturally, he has capitalized on this as well, with a clothing line and a signature "Doggy Biscuitz" sneaker through Pony. His Snoop Dogg Board Company develops skateboards and related clothing.

This unlikely ad pitchman has been paid well to promote T-Mobile, AOL, and Chrysler in TV commercials. Now he has his own record label through Interscope, looking for the next big act to take the baton. One of his albums may have been titled *Paid tha Cost to Be da Bo$$,* but so far being the boss has paid off pretty well for Snoop Dogg.

became the aspiration of anyone who wanted to be larger than life and world famous. In business, icons such as Michael Dell, Jack Welch, Steve Jobs, and Jeff Bezos were often referred to in print as rock stars. But somewhere along the way, rock lost its glamour. Yes, a few rock bands did become true franchises: the Rolling Stones, the biggest, bring in more revenue than many international conglomerates. Classic rock acts, including Jimmy Buffet, have turned decades of concert and album earnings into an enviable fortune.

But where are the brand extensions? Where are the subsidiaries under the larger holding company? Where are the non-music products that sell from Orlando to Osaka? One could argue that rock music created a lifestyle, especially in the 1960s and early 1970s, but from a commercial standpoint, few artists or producers managed to capitalize on it. The hip-hop moguls, on the other hand, did so from the start and turned up the business heat as the music's popularity grew.

The Demographics Have It

Music industry lore pegs the amount of rap music purchased by white consumers at anywhere from 60 percent to 80 percent. Although no scientific studies exist to prove it, most music analysts assume that somewhere between two-thirds to three-quarters of all hip-hop music is bought by white consumers, most of them from the suburbs.

A rap music article in *American Demographics* magazine, published in the mid '90s, when gangsta rap was taking off, said that only 28 percent of teens lived in urban areas. "Inner-city blacks aged 15 to 19 are an even smaller group. At 1.4 million, they are only 8 percent of all teens." Their conclusion was that although rap music would appear to be aimed at inner-city black kids, there was no way the genre would be selling even a fraction of its current numbers if it appealed to only that audience.

If the music is labeled urban or black, it's because the artists and producers are black. As Kenny Burns has said of the upscale RyanKenny clothing line, "The only reason we're considered an 'urban' line is because the owners are black." The appeal of the product certainly goes well beyond the core.

The bottom line: hip-hop is a mainstream, global lifestyle force. Russell Simmons saw that from the start and dreamed big. Sean Combs is dreaming even bigger. Simmons and Combs and the moguls that followed inherently knew that the demographics were on their side. They may have been minorities, but they knew they could extend the hip-hop lifestyle to the majority.

● LL Cool J: Ladies (Still) Love Cool James

James Todd Smith, better known as LL Cool J (for "Ladies Love Cool James"), was one of the original rap music stars. Signed by Russell Simmons in 1984 when he was only a high school teenager, LL was nevertheless an innovator. He was one of the first rappers to use conventional song structure, with a defined chorus, to make rap songs that could be a radio hit. Over a career that has outlasted most pop stars, he has racked up seven platinum and four gold albums.

Along the way, he became even more successful as an actor. He starred in the NBC TV sitcom *In the House* and has been active in several movie roles each year. Some of his most successful films include *Any Given Sunday, Charlie's Angels,* and *S.W.A.T.* In 2005 respected Lions Gate Films signed a multi-year, multi-picture development and production deal to put him behind the camera for nine films.

Long before most rap stars came upon the idea of using their image to sell a clothing line, LL was a partner in a line called Troop in the '80s. In the 1990s he endorsed FUBU, an acronym "For Us, By Us." It conveyed the idea the clothes were made for and by a black person (even if they were, like most current urban lines, manufactured in Asia). With LL appearing in ads and wearing the clothes in videos, sales took off seemingly overnight. He is still active in clothing, but this time with his own namesake: James Todd Smith Clothing.

Ringing in New Lines of Business

Of course like any market, the all-encompassing hip-hop lifestyle market has a saturation point after which growth is going to be difficult. There is already evidence that the urban clothing lines are hitting a wall. Just putting out some club-oriented clothing with a celebrity's name attached isn't the sure bet it used to be. Only so many celebrity energy drinks can succeed on the store shelves. Music sales overall are flat, so stealing market share from other genres can only go so far.

Some up-and-coming moguls are putting their faith in technology. Like Snoop Dogg, several artists and moguls are tapping into downloads, satellite radio, Internet radio, and mobile phone services. The mobile phone ringtone market topped $1 billion globally in 2002, $3.5 billion in 2003, and more than $4 billion in 2004. From the start, the hip-hop crowd saw ringtones as a promotional tool and a way to make an extra buck, not as a cannibalization force to be feared. Dr. Dre and Eminem recognized the power early; they had 50 Cent record ringtones at the same time he recorded his debut album. Now hip-hop rules the *Billboard* ringtones chart; in a typical week, six or seven of the top ten ringtones are from rap artists. On a regular basis, the number one ringtone sells significantly more units than the number one single on the Hot 100 songs.

Jeff Clanagan, founder of Code Black Entertainment is moving into mobile, digital, broadband, and all the other potential applications where consumers are going to want content. "As a content provider, you have to pay attention to the consumer," he says. "If the consumer is telling you he wants two-minute clips on a mobile phone, you better be able to give it to him. If he wants to watch something on a PDA or on a Playstation, you've got to provide it. The consumer is going to dictate whether you are successful or not."

As with all good businesspeople, the current and future hip-hop moguls have their eyes on the bottom line. According to *Business*

Week, operating margins for digital music sales are around 18 percent versus about 12 percent for CDs.

A technological spur to hear the original, raw, graphic street-language lyrics of hip-hop was the advent of Sirius Radio and its competitor XM Radio. Sirius, for example, uses three orbital satellites to broadcast some 120 channels nationwide, with consumers accessing the programming with special receivers and paid by subscription. But why buy something when you can get commercial radio for free? Easy. The FCC, which severely restricts what can be said or sung on commercial radio (read profanity and violent or graphically sexual lyrics), does not impose any such restrictions on programmers such as Sirius. In addition, Sirius offers commercial-free, digital-quality music on more than sixty channels (the rest being devoted to news, sports, weather, TV audio, and the like).

Importantly for hip-hop, SIRIUS devotes five channels to raw and uncensored rap: Hip-Hop Nation (the hits); Backspin (hip-hop classics and oldies); Faction (a mis of punk, hip-hop, and hard rock); Hot Jamz (hip-hop and R&B hits); and Shades 45 (an uncensored hip-hop station created by Sirius and Eminem). Snoop Dogg also DJs on rival XM. (See "Snoop Dogg: From Long Beach Gang Member to Celebrity Icon.") Sirius, flowing the path of many new media, using raw, graphic content to build and audience, expects to have nearly three million subscribers by 2006.

All these new endeavors are logical extensions of what hip-hop has become—an integrated cultural continuum, as opposed to a series of big musical hits. As Atlanta-based black entrepreneur Rodney Sampson points out, "First of all, hip-hop and popular culture is not an *event,* but a *culture* ... most of these hip-hop leaders have maximized their entrepreneurial savvy in the consumer-based marketplace. For instance, most of their products are geared towards the general marketplace that purchases non-appreciating (or depreciating) products such as shoes, clothes, cars, etc. This initial strategy made complete sense, since these consumers were the same persons who were listening to their music."

Paying Forward: Mentoring the Next Generation of Moguls

Another area of expanding influence for the now established hip-hop entrepreneurs is not about the money, it's about mentoring the next generation. Diddy, Simmons, and others make extensive use of interns, mentoring them for the business world. Mentoring has long been a staple of business practice, even formalized into

⟳ The Neptunes, Lil Jon, and Timbaland: The Producer As Branding Machine

Dr. Dre isn't the only one to get in front of the mic, behind the mic, and behind a desk. He won't be the last either. Long before hip-hop came along, the line between producer, artist, and record executive was often a blurry one. From Sinatra to Herb Alpert to Prince, job descriptions were a fluid thing. Hip-hop has amplified this trend and stretched it out. What is new with hip-hop is that the producers become stars in their own right, and they are able to parlay their brand into an empire.

Pharrell Williams, one half of the successful production team known as The Neptunes, is a prime example. *People* magazine listed him as one of the top most-eligible bachelors. In 2005 he took the number one spot on *Esquire* magazine's most stylish list.

He and production partner Chad Hugo can afford a nice wardrobe.

- The two of them are an unstoppable hit machine in the studio, crafting rap tunes for Jay-Z, Missy Elliott, and Snoop Dogg, as well as straight-up pop tunes for Britney Spears, Justin Timberlake, No Doubt, and others.
- They perform with Sheldon "Shay" Haley as N.E.R.D. (No One Ever Really Dies).
- Williams teamed up with Japanese designer Nigo to release the Billionaire Boys Club clothing line and the Ice Cream footwear collection through Reebok.

programs in some mainline businesses. Hip-hop executives are taking it to a new level. Simmons has even taken his advice on the road, giving seminars nationwide about success and financial savvy. As Simmons says:

> Any business out there, if you can be a good intern, you can be a good leader. A good intern is someone who can help someone

- Williams owns the rights to the Fatburger fast-food chain for his native state of Virginia and is in the midst of opening up ten outlets with his partner, former vice president of Walt Disney Pictures, Chris Zarpas.

Lil Jon has learned fast about going from producer to mogul. He has parlayed his own success as an artist and producer (for Usher, Ciara, Ying Yang Twins, Trick Daddy, and others) into options for movie parts, a spot on the world Anger Management rap tour, and production of a sports drink. Like Sean "Diddy" Combs and Damon Dash, Lil Jon has learned that one product line can feed off the other and make both stronger. Both his energy drink and his band's 2005 album were called *Crunk Juice*. "It seems we're jumping 200 feet at a time," he says. And the music comes full circle to the roots: appearing on the album are Ice-T, Ice Cube, and original Def Jam partner and producer Rick Rubin.

Timbaland broke out as a producer in the '90s with a steady stream of innovative tracks for Missy Elliott, the late singer Aaliyah, Jay-Z, and R&B artist Ginuwine. After a while he was getting calls from every major rap and R&B star around, along with rock acts like Beck and Limp Bizkit.

He formed his own label, Beat Club, which did well from the start. He also records and performs as half of Timbaland & Magoo and is a frequent guest rapper on others' recordings. In a partnership with mobile ringtone provider Made Hear, Timbaland launched *Get By*, a "mobile album" of seven specially crafted ringtones—songs made from the start to be played on a small phone speaker.

else make money. If you can help a person be successful in a company that is making money, it's a sign you will be a successful businessperson. The president of a company also has to be a good servant. He has to provide a service to his people to make them feel good about what they're doing. You become a great leader by being a great servant. So there's not much difference in that sense between an intern and the top leader.

Hip-Hop As Conglomerate: Dr. Dre's A-Team

As the money grows, some hip-hop organizations are looking suspiciously like traditional business organizations (though still with an ear to the street instead of in a high-rise.)

Andre "Dr. Dre" Young is a music producer who became an artist almost by accident—first as part of N.W.A., then going solo as the first successful artist for the Death Row label (owned by Dre and Suge Knight). None of that compares to his subsequent earnings as the reigning super-producer of rap; he can be very selective about what he produces, since he reportedly earns $250,000 per song. But now he is also the head of hip-hop's most successful conglomerate.

Dre's empire has all the hallmarks of a well-designed holding company, complete with self-sustaining subsidiaries. His Aftermath Entertainment company includes the Aftermath imprint, Eminem's Shady imprint, and now 50 Cent's G-Unit imprint. The company is also home to Busta Rhymes, Eve, Stat Quo, and The Game.

Dre has proven himself to be a brilliant business leader. He recognized immediately that by giving his star artists their own label, they would treat their own careers and empires more seriously. They would also be able to capitalize on their growing networks and clout, signing acts they could make into stars. The hunch paid off handsomely with Eminem, as he was able to sign 50 Cent and squeeze a song onto the *8 Mile* movie soundtrack right before release. After 50 Cent became a huge success, he set up his G-Unit label under Dre and Eminem's umbrella. G-Unit immediately signed a solid roster of acts, including veterans Mobb Deep and Mase.

Marshall "Eminem" Mathers, a white rapper from Detroit, is *the* hottest artist of the 2000s, in any kind of music. His debut album, *The Marshall Mathers LP,* made him a star from the start. The album sold more than 1.7 million copies its first week and went on to sell seventeen million copies worldwide. His next four releases, including the *8 Mile* movie soundtrack, have all sold at least five million copies in the United States and double that amount worldwide.

So far, however, Eminem's nonmusic ventures have been a mixed bag. The autobiographical movie he starred in, *8 Mile,* was a critical and commercial hit. His clothing line, Shady Ltd., was picked up by several retailers, including Macy's, but sales have charitably been called "slow to take off."

The only artist to be able to counter Eminem's sales dominance in music stores and in downloads has been Curtis "50 Cent" Jackson. After Eminem signed the former gangsta to Shady, he quickly became the best-selling musical artist of the year. His debut album, *Get Rich or Die Tryin',* sold more than seven million copies in the United States alone. The follow-up sold more than one million copies in the first two days.

Jackson's clothing line, G-Unit Clothing Company, reportedly grossed $100 million its first year, according to its manufacturer, Ecko Unlimited. A signature sneaker released through Reebok sold four million pairs. A video game called *50 Cent: Bulletproof* followed, and by the time this book is out, his biopic, *Get Rich or Die Tryin'* will have had a run in the theaters and on DVD.

In a story about 50 Cent, the *New York Daily News* once asked, "How did this kid from Queens, who wasn't worth a nickel, become one of the savviest and wealthiest businessmen in the country?" Perhaps Dr. Dre's business sense rubbed off. In an advertisement for his bottled water brand, Formula 50, a contemplative 50 Cent sits in a white bathrobe, reading the *Wall Street Journal.*

The next level after leading the Hip-Hop Nation? The world, of course!

Hip-Hop Nation to Hip-Hop Planet

Hip-hop is now a global phenomenon. DJs cut and scratch all over the world. Jay-Z, LL, and Fiddy grace ads and billboards from Birmingham, Alabama, to Birmingham, England, from Toledo to Tokyo, and from Vancouver to Valpararíso (Chile). The fashion, slang, and rhythms permeate music and culture on every continent. To classify hip-hop solely as an expression of black American culture misses its growing global reach, cultural power, and economic potential. Hip-hop is a force that is creating a new, worldwide identity. As the UN tries, often in vain, to create a one-world government, hip-hop is a subtereanean force unifying the young of the world.

As Patrick Neate says in his book *Where You're At,* "Some people may not have noticed and some people may not like it, but the truth is we're living on a hip-hop planet."

The Hip-Hop Invasion of Europe

U.S. performers have often done well in Europe, sometimes better than their homegrown talent. Elvis had more number one hits on the U.K. charts (18) than the Beatles (17). Early black singers and jazz musicians from America often found an audience in places like France when they couldn't break through in the United States.

So perhaps it's not surprising that hip-hop took Europe by storm, embracing the genre as fast as the United States did. Sometimes they were even ahead of the curve: Kurtis Blow was a success in the United Kingdom and Holland before blowing up at home. Public Enemy drew bigger crowds on their first European tour than they did on their first American one. There's still a disparity at times today: Eminem has had more number

one singles in England than at home, and half his CD sales have
been from abroad.

PARLEZ-VOUS LE HIP-HOP?

France is the second largest hip-hop market in the world. Rap
has been heard in France since about 1983, with the introduction
of the weekly national television network program *Hip-Hop*. In
1994 the French government, in a bid to fight the onslaught of
English-language pop music, decreed that 40 percent of what was
played on radio stations had to be homegrown talent. "It could
be argued that this law was in part intended to attack hip-hop
and the perceived Americanization of French through its slang,"
says Neate. Ironically, the new law actually benefited French hip-
hop acts the most. That same year, MC Solaar sold more than
a million copies worldwide of his second album, *Prose Combat*.
Now the majority of the French music that sells internationally
is hip-hop music.

MULTILINGUAL RAP GOES PLATINUM

Rap music is prevalent in clubs and car stereos from Portugal
to Bulgaria to Belgium. German versions of gangsta rap now
routinely hit the top ten in album sales. One Italian album by
Articolo 31 sold six hundred thousand copies—a certification of
six times platinum in Italy.

Hip-Hop's Asian Contagion

There are still some parts of Asia that reject all foreign influence—
whatever its nature and wherever it's from. It's viewed as a plague.
And then there are other, large, modern and progressive parts of
Asia that embrace the rest of the global community, accept new
ideas, and, as they've done for centuries, make them their own. It's
true with politics, social issues, management practice, and technology. Nowhere, however, is it more evident than with Western
"cultural" products: movies, music, clothes, and the like.

CULTURAL EXCHANGE

Tokyo has developed a thriving hip-hop scene with both commercial and underground currents. Party rap appeals to teenage girls, and underground hip-hop appeals to teenage boys, opposing the rigid traditional mainstream. In any case, the music itself is almost secondary. In Japan it's hip-hop fashion that is the real star. Tokyo is a hot market for Phat Farm, Sean John, and Rocawear; whatever clothing is on display in U.S. rap videos and in magazines is sure to be all over the streets and clubs of Japan soon after. The Japanese culture of appropriation has effortlessly swallowed hip-hop.

Elsewhere in Asia, rap seems initially to have been incorporated into the existing repertoires of pop singers, largely as one of many Western popular musical idioms, with little specialization in rap music or hip-hop culture. Rap becomes an element in Thai music, Hindi music, or gets mixed with Korean folk songs. In the meantime, rappers from the United States find a receptive audience there, whether the lyrics are understood or not.

But it's not all a one-way street. Asia has also influenced U.S. hip-hop culture in the form of martial arts and kung fu, which U.S. hip-hop groups like the Wu-Tang Clan have embraced.

Hip-Hop's Latin Lovers

American Latinos participated in the early days of rap in the South Bronx, and the rest of Latin America quickly embraced hip-hop's message of disaffection. In Brazil, Raciones MC's album *Sobrevivendo No Inferno* sold more than a million commercial copies (and probably three or four times that many bootlegs). In Mexico, Control Machete's first album, *Mucho Barato*, went platinum in Mexico, selling some three hundred thousand units, surprising American hip-hop business executives with the notion of a thriving Mexican rap scene.

Rampant piracy and high commercial CD prices make an accurate picture in this region difficult. However, anyone who travels through the cities of Latin America will hear rap music blasting from nearly any corner kiosk and will see hip-hop fashion out in full force.

Africa: Hip-Hop Comes Full Circle

The roots of rap are in Africa, and the form has understandably taken off right were it was born. (Senegal's Daara J titled one album *Boomerang*.) As the liner notes to the album *Global Hip-Hop* inform us, "In Africa it's by far the most popular youth music and, as Frada Freddy from Senegalese band Daara J points out, there are over 6,000 hip-hop groups in Dakar alone." Compilations such as *Rough Guide to African Rap* and *Red Hot & Riot* have brought African acts to a global audience.

South Africa's rap scene is the most developed. It even has it's own hip-hop clothing company, Loxion Kulca. Following the rap mogul blueprint, they encourage rappers to wear their gear and instead of hiring lots of designers, they encourage individuals to set up subsidiaries under the parent company.

Global Hip-Hop: From the Sub-Sahara to the South Bronx to Bejing and Back

Hip-hop's roots are African, its modern expression as a cultural and economic force is American, but its destiny is global. The compilation album called *Global Hip-Hop* contains recordings from Chile, Nigeria, Turkey, Lebanon, Mexico, and India. *Business 2.0* magazine profiled an American entrepreneur named Andrew Ballen who had started staging hip-hop nights at clubs in Shanghai, China. The nights were a smash success. After four years, he has raked in $2 million, gets lucrative ad pitchman offers, and has his own hip-hop TV show and radio show.

Today, the music is everywhere, perhaps being the world's first global music. It's spilling out of the projects and barrios, barrooms and back lots, and onto the main streets of the world. But it's not just the music that's spreading, it's bringing with it the entire set of cultural products and social ethos that hip-hop engenders.

The influences are flowing back and forth as well, forming something new. Wyclef Jean was a rapper (alongside Lauren Hill) with the Fugees, a band whose album *The Score* sold more than seventeen million copies worldwide in the mid '90s. After a decade of success as a solo artist and producer, his fifth solo album, *Creole 101 (Welcome to Haiti)*, is a nod to his Haitian birthplace. Most of the songs are in Haitian creole. The music he makes, combining elements of both worlds, is altogether new.

As a truly worldwide phenomenon, hip-hop will define and direct much of the social mores and global cultural consciousness of the generation about to seize political power from the baby-boomer generation. As that earlier generation embraced rock and the values of the '60s, so too will those who embrace the hip-hop planet. They will influence the world's political and social agenda for decades to come.

Future Challenges: "What's Really Next?"

As it approaches its thirtieth birthday, hip-hop is now at a natural crossroads. With the success the music and lifestyle is enjoying, can the genre keep growing? Can the hip-hop collective find new markets to conquer? Many in the black community are also saying it's time to start playing a different tune, one that doesn't rely on the mythical thuggish black man, celebrated for committing crime and abusing women. Kanye West appears to be one who closely fits the bill.

Along the way, there have been bumps in the road. Many of rap's earlier stars signed bad deals that left them broke when the fame faded. A few labels have come and gone, either because of falling sales or because of contractual problems. (Master P let his No Limit label go bankrupt rather than keeping it alive just to fend off old lawsuits.) As the business has matured, it has gotten more serious and more business-like.

Kanye West:
The College Dropout Graduates to the Big Time

When you ask those in the know who will be the next Russell Simmons or Diddy, or at least the next Jay-Z, the name Kanye West is usually the one that comes up. His second album, *Late Registration*, sold 860,000 copies in its first week. He graced the cover of *Time* magazine that same week and appeared in a Pepsi ad directed by Spike Lee soon after.

Kanye West is one of the few rappers in history who was a multimillionaire before his first single hit the streets. He had already made it big as a producer, working on tracks for Alicia Keys, Jay-Z, and Ludacris while still in high school.

His debut album, *The College Dropout*, was a critical and sales sensation. Instead of violent thug-life clichés and put-downs, it featured intelligent raps, a nod to God, and a tirade against showy materialism. Jay-Z has often been called the franchise of Roc-A-Fella, but Kanye West surely complicated that story. He sold several million copies of his freshman album, just as Jay-Z and Damon Dash's Roc-A-Fella label was folded into Def Jam. Three of his singles were hits in a long list of countries. Along with Jay-Z, West was named one of the most influential people in the world in *Time* magazine's annual "Time 100" list. West also became the most-nominated artist at the 2005 Grammy Awards, with ten nominations for his own album and production work for Alicia Keys and Janet Jackson. He eventually went home with three awards, the first of many from a variety of shows.

Kanye West didn't waste any time in branching out. Often making the "best-dressed" lists, he has his own clothing line—Pastel Clothing. His record label is called G.O.O.D. Music (Getting Out Our Dreams), which was home to a platinum album from John Legend and the critically acclaimed *Be* from the artist Common. Many in the industry are hoping G.O.O.D. Music can bring rap back to the style of the early '90s, when conscious raps and sales success weren't mutually exclusive.

What's in Their DNA?: Rappin' It Up

All businesses, all industries, *with no exceptions,* go in cycles: from inception and growth, to maturity and decline. The same is true for technologies, products, companies, and brands, and even management styles and practice.

Some follow the cycle to decline and death like lemmings going over a cliff. Others, however, discover the final secret of long-term business success. Actually it's not really much of a secret. It's discussed every day in every boardroom and on every factory floor, and it can be summed up in one word: change.

The one true ultimate lesson of business success is the need for constant change, or as they call it in business school, *strategic renewal.* That is, stripping away what made a company successful and finding a new way to sell, manufacture, ship, engage customers, use a new technology, find a new niche, or any of the other myriad new ways that companies find to be successful over long periods of time.

Some companies have done it in a revolutionary fashion, like IBM in the late 1990s, with almost blinding speed, seemingly "retooling" their enterprise in a matter of days. Others change slowly over time, making slow evolutionary but continual changes that are almost imperceptible. General Electric (GE) is the undisputed master of the latter: change is in their DNA. They never make any sudden moves, but over a period time they make a slow, steady transformation in their businesses, management processes, and sources of revenue and profits. GE is the *only* company to be in the top ten largest American enterprises in the years 1900 *and* 2000.

Whether or not the hip-hop enterprises survive and thrive or wither and die is a matter for the history books. Only time will tell. What we do know, however, is that the hip-hop business world will follow the path that is familiar to every other business.

Promising but undercapitalized businesses will fail. Poorly marketed brands will quietly fade away. Brand extensions will fail.

There will be leadership changes at the top. There will be IPOs, consolidations, mergers, and acquisitions. The profit margins will get tighter, and the CEOs will have to watch the bottom line more closely. The fickle tastes of Hollywood will change once again. The business will mature, and some will decline into shadows of their former greatness.

Today's thirty-something hip-hop consumers will someday be in their sixties and seventies. Will they still wear their hats crooked, their beltless baggy pants hanging down to their knees, hi-top laces untied? Will their cars still have spinners and their evening wear include a mountain of bling?

There can be no doubt that today's hip-hop businesses will undergo change. That is a given. What is left to the unknown is how they will respond to the changes that will surely come. They may survive; they may disappear. But whatever happens, the rest of their story needs to be told. Regardless of the outcome, they truly deserve the attention. Perhaps some will eventually be the subject of a business case.

Yo, Harvard. Are you listening?

INDEX